CHARITABLE REMAINDER TRUSTS

CHARITABLE REMAINDER TRUSTS

A Proven Strategy for Reducing Estate and Income Taxes through Charitable Giving

Peter J. Fagan, CLU, ChFC

SM

International Association for Financial Planning

IRWIN
Professional Publishing

Chicago • Bogotá • Boston • Buenos Aires • Caracas
London • Madrid • Mexico City • Sydney • Toronto

The International Association for Financial Planning (IAFP) is an organization dedicated to the idea that objective advice supports smart financial decisions. The IAFP represents more than 12,000 individuals and institutions in all 50 states who believe that financial planning is the foundation for smart decision-making. The IAFP is the only industry-wide organization in the financial services industry. Established in 1969, it provides its members with education, training, products and services to promote its member's professionalism and success. With over 110 chapters throughout the United States, it works to build public awareness of the importance of achieving financial independence. For further information, call 1–800–945–4237.

This publication is designed to provide accurate and authoritative information in regard to the subject matter covered. It is sold with the understanding that neither the author or the publisher is engaged in rendering legal, accounting, or other professional service. If legal advice or other expert assistance is required, the services of a competent professional person should be sought.

From a Declaration of Principles jointly adopted by a Committee of the American Bar Association and a Committee of Publishers.

Irwin Professional Book Team

Executive editor: *Amy Hollands Gaber*
Production supervisor: *Dina L. Treadaway*
Assistant manager, desktop services: *Jon Christopher*
Project editor: *Waivah Clement*
Senior designer: *Larry J. Cope/Becky Gordon*
Jacket designer: *Concialdi Design*
Compositor: *Wm. C. Brown Publishers*
Typeface: *11/13 Palatino*
Printer: *Maple-Vail Book Manufacturing Group*

Times Mirror
Higher Education Group

Library of Congress Cataloging-in-Publication Data

Fagan, Peter J.
    Charitable remainder trusts: a proven strategy for reducing estate and income taxes through charitable giving / Peter J. Fagan.
        p.   cm.
    Includes bibliographical references and index.
    ISBN 0–7863–0229–1
    1. Income tax deductions for charitable contributions—United States. 2. Charitable uses, trusts, and foundations—Taxation—United States. 3. Tax planning—United States. I. Title.
KF6388.F34 1996
343.7305'23—dc20
[347.303523]   95–22443

Printed in the United States of America
1 2 3 4 5 6 7 8 9 0 MP 2 1 0 9 8 7 6 5

This endeavor is dedicated to my lovely wife and partner, Janet. Without her understanding, compassion, and moral support, it would never have been brought to fruition.

Preface

A number of Internal Revenue Tax Code changes over the last decade or so have severely restricted the breadth and scope of individual income tax deductions available to American taxpayers. These changes continue unabated today.

One area that has survived this onslaught of new and increased activity is the charitable deduction, in particular the charitable remainder trust deduction. As advisors seek available avenues to assist their clients in maximizing the use of their assets, discussions on charitable trusts are becoming more and more frequent.

Many articles concerning charitable remainder trusts have recently appeared in trade journals and general publications. Many of these are somewhat confusing, highly technical, and sometimes contradictory. Most of those writing articles do not specialize in this area. In this book, I intend to demystify charitable trusts by making their uses understandable, simplifying the approaches, pointing out their many benefits, and explaining what they can and cannot do. Included in the discussion will be a number of detailed examples of their use.

The general theme of this book is to view charitable trusts, in particular charitable remainder trusts, as vehicles for converting individual financial situations that are normally viewed as negative into positive financial situations. Charitable trusts are viewed from two perspectives: the donor's and the charity's. Charitable trusts are never enacted in a vacuum. There are always overriding issues and considerations, both from charitable and tax-planning perspectives.

By best estimates, between 3 and 5 percent of the charities in the United States are currently the beneficiaries of charitable trusts. The remaining 90-odd percent of charities for the most part lack the capability or wherewithal to develop these types of gifts. This is primarily due to the lack of properly trained staff in the development area or the lack of commitment of funds necessary to attract these types of gifts. Often, donors do not consider these organizations as recipients of these type of gifts.

The need for the financial solvency of our charitable organizations is more critical today than ever. Both society and the government are calling upon these organizations to take on an ever-growing agenda. The establishment of endowments and the supplementing of current operating budgets is vital. Charitable trusts can play a key role in fulfilling those needs.

Americans, by their very nature, are generous people. Ask them to give of their time or money and many will respond. Ask them to include as part of their income and estate tax planning a charitable trust and some will respond. Change the emphasis of this request, educate and show how all parties (the donor, the charity, society, and the government) benefit from the creation of a charitable trust, and many more will respond.

Quite often, a charity will address fund-raising from the gift-giving perspective. This can take the form of a gift today or one in the future. Financial advisors rarely start with a charitable gift directly in mind. Rather, they start with client needs and desires in mind. That is not to say that the charity does not have the donor in mind, but that their initial approach can be significantly different than that of the financial advisor.

What information can the advisor provide clients that will benefit their current financial situation? This information needs to clarify their financial position. With better understanding of charitable trusts and their unique uses and advantages, this advice can be more meaningful and beneficial. By combining a client's financial needs with the needs of the charitable community and society at large, an interesting and exciting synergism can develop.

This is happening everywhere in the United States. Take, for example, the city of Indianapolis. Anyone visiting this city can't help but notice the many modern structures and the redevelopment of the inner city that has occurred. All of the this was done without any federal dollars. It was done with private charitable dollars from local organizations and individuals interested in bettering their community both for themselves and for all the other citizens. Examples such as this abound throughout the country.

With the recent advent of publicity surrounding charitable trusts, many instant experts have appeared on the scene. In the past, installation and maintenance of a charitable trust was a costly and often onerous task. Today it is much easier. However, it is still technically complex. There are many tax traps awaiting the unprepared and ill-advised. Quite often, the instant expert falls victim to these traps.

Many advisors concentrate on the deductibility of charitable trusts as their primary client motivation. Often, although the deduction is important, it is not the primary motivating factor. There are other considerations that can be as or more important: charitable motivations, tax-free asset conversions, and tax-exempt accumulations, just to name a few. By being fully aware of all aspects of these trusts, advisors can be better prepared to assist their clients.

By acquiring a better understanding and a working knowledge of charitable trusts, an advisor can be prepared to identify specific client situations where a discussion of a charitable trust can be initiated. Once an initial discussion has been concluded and an interest generated, it is advisable to gain the assistance of a professional. This professional should be well versed in the idiosyncrasies of charitable giving and charitable trusts.

Quite often, the charitable trust solution to a given situation is dismissed before it is ever presented to a client. The reason for this is that the advisor, rightly or wrongly, assumes that the client is not charitably motivated. Many people, however, once they are exposed to the merits of a charitable trust and understand their flexibility are motivated to discuss a possible implementation in their own situation. With the use of an expanded understanding of client motivations regarding charitable gifts, the advisor can render valuable service both to the client and society at large.

Another area where the charitable trust can be an innovative and flexible tool is with estate taxes. Over the next 30 years, somewhere between 8 to 10 trillion dollars of assets are going to pass from the generation over age 55 to the next. The size of this intergenerational transfer is unparalleled in the history of the world. Creative solutions to the impact of estate taxes on the assets being transferred have to be found. One area where an advisor can help the client is in understanding the impact of charitable giving and charitable trusts on estate planning.

The reality is that eventually we are all going to die. When we do, there are basically only three things that can happen to our assets: They can go to the heirs, after taxes; they can go to the government in the form of taxes (involuntary contributions to society); or they can be directed to an interest of the client (voluntary contributions to society). Most people would rather make a gift and decide the beneficiary than pay a tax and have the government decide. An advisor who fully understands the impact of charitable trusts in estate planning can have a major impact on the client's situation. There are few other situations in financial and estate planning that provide such an opportunity.

It is my intention in writing this book to provide an explanation, a summary, and a format that allows advisors and/or clients to acquire information needed to make an intelligent decision regarding their financial situation and the use of charitable trust agreements. Such an informed decision, when properly acted upon, can have a dramatic impact on both the client and society.

"What you spend is gone. What you keep, someone else gets. What you give is yours forever."

Dr. Wil Rose

Peter J. Fagan

ACKNOWLEDGMENTS

No project of this nature can be accomplished in a vacuum. The aid and assistance of a number of people helped to bring this project to successful completion. I would in particular like to thank Larraine Zwang for her unwavering perseverance and outstanding editorial assistance and to Jean Armstrong for her valuable input and technical competence. My thanks to Harry Ballard for his diligence. Special appreciation to the folks at Irwin Professional Publishing: Amy H. Gabor, Waivah Clement, and Brian Hayes. In particular, my deepest thanks to Pamela Sourelis for an extraordinary editing effort.

P. J. F.

CONTENTS

Chapter One

The Dynamics of Charitable Giving in the United States

THE HISTORY OF PHILANTHROPY IN THE UNITED STATES

In no other country does charitable giving exist in the magnitude that it does here in the United States. Yet few of us are aware of the huge impact that charitable giving has on our day-to-day lives. The record of accomplishments of American philanthropists is so impressive that it would take volumes to list its achievements.[1]

The history of charitable giving in the United States can be traced back to our Founding Fathers. The first amendment of the U.S. Constitution states the following: "Congress shall make no law respecting an establishment of religion or prohibiting the free exercise thereof; or abridging the freedom of speech, or of the press; or the right of the people to peacefully assemble and to petition the government for a redress of grievances."

This guaranteed right "to voluntarily associate with others to promote the public good" was unique to our Constitution and became the hallmark of our democracy. This 18th-century idealism, developed by the framers of our Constitution, continued the earlier traditions of 17th-century America as emphasized by Cotton Mather, a Massachusetts cleric, when he announced that "Boston's helpfulness and readiness to do every good work were well and favorably known in heaven."[2]

Since our nation's earliest days, Americans have thought of themselves as highly philanthropic. This spirit has continued into modern times. In 1917, Congress adopted an act that introduced the first income tax to the United States. It was no accident that at the same time Congress also enacted the first income tax deduction. Thus was created the first tax-deductible charitable contribution. These deductible contributions had to be made to organizations devoted exclusively to charity, religion, education, science, or the prevention of cruelty to animals or children. Our founding fathers in the 1700s and the U.S. House of Representatives and the Senate in the early part of the 20th century affirmed, by their actions, philanthropy's place in America.

Philanthropy, this hallmark of our democracy, is constantly being reaffirmed in that role. J. D. Livingston, Chairman of INTERPHIL, stated that "INTERPHIL (The International Standing Conference on Philanthropy) is convinced that modern philanthropy is a buttress to and a pivot for the practice of democracy. Where democracy thrives, philanthropy thrives. Where philanthropy thrives, democracy will thrive." He further said that "modern philanthropy is the process whereby gifts of goods, services and money are applied to altruistic purposes and recognized by the state as operating exclusively for that purpose."[3]

MODERN DAY AMERICAN PHILANTHROPY

With this background, let us look at philanthropy in the 1990s in America. INTERPHIL, in a recent international survey, ranks the United States in a category of its own in regard to its tax treatment of contributions and charitable activities. They report that the tax treatment of donors is most generous and that the tax treatment of charities is exceptionally liberal.[4] Few countries in Western Europe, most with many of the same traditions that molded our founders, score well in the survey. The exceptions are the United Kingdom, Germany, and Greece. In fact, most of them offer few or no tax incentives to donors. In other parts of the world, Israel, Japan, Canada, and Australia score well. The shining example, however, is the United States.

Tax law and charitable contributions have become very involved and interconnected. The individual taxpayer making a contribution to a charitable organization must not only ponder the charitable intent, but also the tax impact and consequences. Congress and the Internal Revenue Service continually revise many of the rules pertaining to a variety of charitable gifts. This constant tinkering with the regulations quite often creates situations where the timing of the gift is critical to the tax deductibility. These constant changes make the services of a professional advisor virtually mandatory in most large charitable gift situations. It can certainly be argued that without the ability to deduct their charitable contributions from their income and estate taxes, Americans would not be as generous as they are currently. There are, however, a number of sides to this argument.

TAX EXEMPT ORGANIZATIONS

There are currently over one million tax exempt, 501(c) organizations in the United States, and over 60 percent of these are charitable. These organizations employ almost 7 percent of the U.S. workforce, approximately eight million people.[5] The annual budgets for charitable organizations in the 1990s will average over $500 billion. Twenty-five percent of this total, $125 billion, is raised from charitable donations. Contrary to popular belief, over 80 percent of this total is contributed by individual donors. In 1973, total giving in the United States amounted to $25 billion; over the last two decades there has been an average annual increase of 4 percent.[6]

These figures are certainly impressive. Measuring the impact of the employees of the various charitable organizations and the expenditures from these charities on the day-to-day lives of the American people is an enormous task. The nonprofit sector of the American economy has tremendous influence and responsibility, which the federal government fully recognizes. Just imagine what would happen to our tax structure if charities ceased to exist or their funding was drastically curtailed by changes in giving patterns based upon modifications in the tax law. Who would provide the replacement services? How high would tax rates go?

SOURCES OF CONTRIBUTIONS

The sources of contributions to charitable entities have remained fairly constant over the last decade. Of the total cited above, almost 82 percent of contributions come directly from individual donors. Approximately 6 percent of the totals comes from testamentary bequests and wills. The remaining 12 percent is divided between foundation contributions at 7 percent and corporate contributions at 5 percent. It is therefore quite apparent that charitable organizations depend significantly on the generosity of the individual.[7]

Many people believe that wealthy individuals give the preponderance of charitable contributions. Naturally, their dollar amount is significant, but the majority of dollars are contributed by poor and middle-class households. Since these families account for an overwhelming percentage of the U.S. population, the magnitude of these total dollar contributions is enormous. In fact, households earning under $20,000 annually contribute at 4.8 percent, the largest share of household income. Households with income range between $75,000 and $99,000 follow closely behind, at 4.5 percent of income. These figures go a long way toward discounting the argument that charitable contributions would dry up if the tax deductibility were removed. Americans by their very nature are a generous people.

The actual average amount per household extrapolated from the 1990 census is $978. Age is another factor. As one might suspect, those under 24 contribute approximately one-half the average amount. The largest average contribution coincides with the latter part of the peak earning years, ages 55 to 64, at 145 percent of the national averages. As can be seen, the average dollars per household are not enormous, but taken as a whole, the sum is significant.[8]

DISTRIBUTION OF CONTRIBUTIONS

Where do all the contributions go? These percentage breakdowns have also remained fairly consistent year in and year out over the last decade. Not surprisingly, over 45 percent of all dollars raised go to religious organizations. The next largest category is education at 11 percent, with higher education receiving the substantial portion of these gifts. Next is the area of services at a little over 9 percent of the total. Health areas are the next greatest receivers at 8 percent. This is very closely followed by arts, culture, and the humanities at 7.5 percent. Public and social benefit areas receive over 4 percent of the contributions. The last two measurable categories are environment and wildlife at 2.5 percent and international affairs at 1.4 percent. The remaining 10 percent of contributions goes to areas amounting to less than 1 percent of the total and to otherwise unspecified categories.[9]

From the religious giving total of $56 billion to the international affairs segment at $175 million, the impact upon our daily lives of charitable contributions is only partially measured. The dollar totals do not begin to reflect the countless hours that large numbers of citizens volunteer to many organizations. There is no certifiable method of measuring this total nor of assessing its dollar value. If this could be done, this figure would easily pale the $125 billion contribution total. This can be borne out by simple observation in every community in America. Many individuals are giving of their time to more than one worthy organization. The spirit of our founders is alive and thriving in every corner of America in the 1990s.

EVOLUTION OF PLANNED GIVING

As our income and estate tax law has changed and evolved since 1917, so has the idea of charitable giving, especially the area of planned giving. The basic definition of *planned giving* is any charitable giving into which a thought process is interjected into the formulation of the gift. It would be difficult to clearly establish which came first, the changes in giving or the revisions in the tax law. As can be found in other areas of tax law, rules and regulations are created and adapted to correspond to ongoing circumstances. At the same time, innovative techniques are developed to utilize the provisions of tax law.

This same type of evolution most likely takes place in a number of planned gift-giving arrangements into which donors enter. They normally start out with a purpose for the gift that may or may not have an altruistic move. Income and/or estate tax considerations will quite often be combined with charitable intent. As the gift-giving process unfolds, the reasoning for the creation of the gift quite often evolves onto a totally different plane. Normally, once an individual donor becomes more intimately involved with a charitable organization through a planned giving process, the psychological and emotional aspects of charitable gift giving replace the more mundane numbers-oriented attitudes.

Planned giving has slowly evolved among charitable organizations. The number of charities with full-time planned giving staff is still relatively small in relation to the total number of organizations. Fewer than 10 percent of all charitable organizations have full-time planned giving staff.

Recent tax acts, in particular the tax act of 1986, have codified various charitable planned giving techniques. With such codification, the government has done much to encourage the establishment of these types of charitable gifts. The 1969 Tax Act brought with it the creation of the charitable remainder trust (CRT).[10] This formalized the concept that had been previously known as a life income arrangement. In so doing, the government brought forth an extremely interesting and exciting planned giving idea, with significant income and estate tax consequences favorable to the donor. With this further sanction of a very useful income and estate planning tool, the modern course of charitable planned giving was launched. It has taken a number of years since the enactment of this section of the Internal Revenue Code for a full understanding of its varied uses to be broadly disseminated to the financial advisory community.

Planned giving, which had been relegated to a secondary role, started to take on added importance as more charitable organizations began to understand the need to establish endowment funds to help with future operational costs and to lessen the almost 100 percent dependence on annual contributions. Many charitable organizations discovered that in order to accomplish a large project, such as a capital campaign, incorporating planned giving became essential. Planned giving arrangements and techniques were much more fully investigated, not only by the planned giving community itself, but also by the financial advisory profession as a means of addressing client financial problems.

Added to this was a major shift in the 1980s to higher overall marginal income and estate tax rates, resulting in a further impetus to charitable gift planning. Today, with significantly fewer deductions than were available in the past, marginal federal income tax rates are approaching 50 percent. Add to this the state taxes in some of the higher income tax states, and overall rates can reach as high as 60 percent. Federal estate and gift tax rates, effective after each taxpayer's $600,000 lifetime exemption, start at 37 percent and quickly escalate to 55 percent. Again, in a number of states, the addition of state inheritance and estate taxes can add 4–7 percent to these rates. All of this contributes to a new awareness of charitable income and estate tax planned giving.

SOCIAL CAPITAL

Most conventional thinking would characterize the 1980s as the "decade of greed." This prevailing mode of thought was reinforced by the network news-analysis segments. Yet in reality the 1980s was a decade in which the rate of growth in charitable giving was 55 percent higher than in the previous 25 years and private philanthropy in the United States was the highest in the history of man.[11]

As was evident in the 1980s, there are also major paradigm shifts that are taking place in this decade. Are there shifts that we can identify that are going to have a major long-term and lasting impact on the development of society?

One change that is readily discernible is the aging of the population of the industrialized countries, which has created many social concerns. In the United States, for example, in 1940 only 2 percent of the federal budget was allocated to those over age 65. In 1989, that figure had increased to almost 27 percent. Current allocations will bring that total to over 30 percent by the turn of the century. The strain that these expenditures will put on federal and state budgets will have an enormous impact on their overall tax structure.

The senior segment of the population is one of the fastest-growing segments in the country. In fact, those over age 85 represent the fastest-growing age bracket. This growth is occurring without the arrival of the Baby Boomer generation into the ranks of the senior population. Once the 56 million Baby Boomers start to reach normal retirement age, the ranks of the senior population are going to swell dramatically. This is occurring at the same time as the total number of younger people comprising the working population and called upon to support the expenditures for Social Security and Medicare is on the decline.

Not only is this percentage of the population growing, but they, along with the generation immediately succeeding them, have accumulated a large percentage of the personal wealth in this country. Individuals over age 55 in the United States are estimated to control somewhere between 8–10 trillion dollars of personal assets. This is a significant sum and one that will play a larger and larger role in the overall tax scenario as government resources are more stringently allocated. Such a large sum will hardly escape the increased tax reach of the watchful politician or bureaucrat.

In recent years, successive federal administrations, along with the United States Treasury Department, have invoked estate and succession taxation policies that have made it much more difficult to pass assets from one generation to the next. This trend in taxation and regulation will certainly not abate in light of current federal budgetary restraints. In addition, deceased citizens, except in a few very isolated localities, are not a voting constituency that has to be appeased.

Another definitive trend we Americans are experiencing is in the makeup of our population growth. Ethnicities in the United States that have for years been classified as minorities, are now the fastest-growing segment of the population and, combined, will some time in the early part of the 21st century constitute the majority of the population. This by itself is a major paradigm shift that we are only starting to understand. The upcoming social, cultural, and financial changes will be a major development over the first few decades of the next century.

Another trend is the increasing impact of the computer on our daily lives. Since its initial development, the ability of the microchip to process information has doubled every 18 months. At present, there is no end in sight to this arithmetic progression. The dramatic rise in the use of the personal computer has also greatly changed both social and business interactions. Today, the ability of the individual to access, process, and utilize information on an almost instantaneous basis is virtually unlimited.

As the processing power of the microchip continues to grow, its impact on society will continue to increase and expand. It is difficult to fully comprehend the changes that are being brought about by that small piece of silicon. The status quo in every area is constantly being challenged. In many respects, after the initial years of development, government never had any major influence on the computer industry and has basically been ineffective in its attempts to exercise any control or have a major impact. Each attempt to exercise a degree of control or to restrain the industry has been met with great reluctance and has resulted in a transfer of influence from the government to the industry itself.

A somewhat bothersome trend that has been developing over the last two decades and that has accelerated in the current one is the feeling of a growing segment of the population that the American Dream has passed them by. There is an accelerating sense in certain segments of our population that their lives will never be as good as their parents'. As can be seen in any major city and a number of smaller ones, a portion of the population have dropped out of society, either at an early age during high school or some time later. Many of these individuals end up putting significant strains on the resources of government and the charitable sector to respond to their needs. Quite often, they feel that the government doesn't represent them and that they have been left out by the system.

At the same time, perhaps one of the most significant countering trends is the increase in activism on the part of many individual citizens and citizen groups. There is an ever-growing awareness that it is up to the individual citizens of the country to address the problems of society, that government and money alone are not the solution to many of our social problems. This newfound activism is exemplified in the area of personal finances by an ever-increasing awareness of a concept of *social capital.*

Social capital is embodied in the idea that the individual can and should exercise a large degree of control over his or her own capital in a manner previously little known and underutilized.

As Americans in the 1990s rekindle a strong sense of community and a spirit of involvement in an atmosphere of heightened concern regarding "big government," the concept of social capital is one that can be easily assimilated.

This concept basically divides personal capital into two parts: financial capital and social capital. Personal financial capital is that part of your earnings and assets that you and your family consume, combined with the part that you accumulate for yourself and your heirs. Personal social capital is that part of your earnings and assets that either is extracted by the government in the form of taxes or is given away by you in the form of donations, either while alive or at death, to charitable organizations.

This can also be viewed as government directed philanthropy (involuntary philanthropy) and self-directed philanthropy (voluntary philanthropy). An additional means of expressing this is to view capital as having two parts: the part that you and your family can keep and the part that you and your family cannot keep. A major tenet of the social capital doctrine is that of voluntary and involuntary philanthropy. If we start to view our taxes as philanthropic contributions, a major change in psyche takes place.

Our current tax climate requires us to part, both annually and at death, with a portion of the assets we have earned or saved. Under our progressive system of taxation, the more we earn or save, the larger the percentage of the tax. The system, in order to be successful, requires the voluntary cooperation of the majority of the country's citizens. In a voluntary system, we have choices. One of the choices that can be exercised is to structure our financial affairs to pay the least amount of taxes legally permissible. These taxes that are collected are redistributed according to federal allocations for the common good. We know what happens to the part we keep, and we think we know what happens to the part we cannot keep. But do we really?

Let us review how the monies collected through the tax system are distributed by the federal government (see Exhibit 1–1). As you review the percentage distributions, focus on how this allocation of your dollars actually reflects your personal views and

EXHIBIT 1–1
Where Do Your Federal Dollars Go?

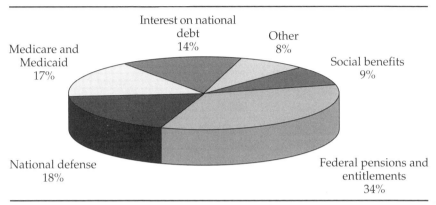

Interest on national
debt
14%

Other
8%

Medicare and
Medicaid
17%

Social benefits
9%

National defense
18%

Federal pensions and
entitlements
34%

Source: Averages of recent U.S. budgets over the last few years.

values. How much of the dollars collected are actually spent on programs that are of interest to you and your family? How many of your dollars are actually returned to your local community in ways that express and amplify your views?

Many U.S. citizens live in net loss states for federal tax purposes; that is, more dollars leave the state in federal tax payments than are returned to those individual states in federally supported programs. How much of the actual tax dollars that you and your family expend will actually be returned to your community? This is an important question to ask and one that most individuals can only vaguely answer. One of the major redistributions of wealth among different areas of the country takes place through this process.

The budget allocations reflect a redistribution of tax dollars based upon a federal agenda. We may or may not agree with that agenda. If each of us could direct this redistribution of our tax dollars, we most likely would not develop the same allocation as the federal government. For example, we are all aware that the threat of a communist takeover of Western Europe has been dramatically reduced. Yet the federal government is still allocating more tax revenues for the defense of Western Europe than it expends for the environment, children, education, infrastructure, and civilian research and development combined. In addition to these types of allocations, a large percentage of tax revenues is consumed by the bureaucracy and is wasted. We are all aware of the federal waste horror stories that appear all too often in the local and national media.

This portion of our wealth that is redistributed by government has been termed *involuntary philanthropy,* in effect, making all of us philanthropists. As was emphasized earlier, this is a very important concept. The dollars that are being redistributed by the government are ours, and we should influence much more control on how those dollars are utilized. Unfortunately, many Americans view the national government as some nebulous body over which they have little or no influence. Hopefully through individual initiative this view will change.

Remember, we are talking about dollars you are going to lose. They cannot be retained; they are gone. You or your family cannot spend or save them. These are also dollars that most likely are not going to be returned in full to your state or community. Even if they are, they will probably not be allocated to programs that express the interests or values of you and your family. Why not put them to use in areas that you and your family are vitally interested in?

Just imagine if these wasted dollars could be recaptured from Washington and expended in your community on causes that interest you and your family. What impact would that have on you, your family, and your community? A major redirection of social capital to your local communities and your special interests can start to transform the future of this country in ways totally unimaginable to anyone.

This is a major paradigm shift!

If you were given $1 million tomorrow and you could not spend it or save it or invest it or give it to your family or friends, what would you do with it?

Chapter Two

Gifting Techniques

FEDERAL TAX TREATMENT

Before we begin a discussion of various planned giving techniques, it will be helpful to review the federal tax treatment of the deductibility of charitable contributions.

In order for individual taxpayers to deduct charitable contributions for income tax purposes, they must first have the ability to itemize deductions.[1] If they cannot itemize, any charitable contributions are lumped into their standard deduction.

There are two further qualifications for deductibility. First, the maximum percentage offset of 50 percent of total deductions may limit the actual impact of the charitable deduction.[2] Second, a further qualification to deductibility is that the gift must be made to a charity recognized by the IRS.[3] Section 501(c)(3) of the Internal Revenue Code details the qualification rules for the charities. All Section 501(c)(3) organizations are listed in a federal registry, commonly referred to as the Blue Book.[4]

Charitable contributions are deductible up to a percentage of adjusted gross income, dependent upon the type of asset donated to the organization or, as in the case of a private foundation, the type of organization. The overall maximum any individual taxpayer can deduct from income in one tax year is 50 percent of adjusted gross income.[5] All deductions that are not usable in a current tax year may be carried forward for five more years and deducted as the availability of the deduction occurs.[6]

For estate tax purposes, all charitable gifts to organizations recognized by Section 501(c)(3) are deductible from the gross estate. There is no limit on the amount or percentage of the assets that may be given to a qualified charitable organization and deducted from the gross estate.[7]

The final category of tax that affects gifts is the gift tax. In order to be deductible for gift tax purposes, charitable gifts must be made to organizations that are qualified recipients for that purpose.[8]

TYPES OF GIFTS

The basic definition of a planned gift is one that requires thought and a degree of involvement on the part of the donor. This degree of involvement can be modest or quite extensive. A planned gift can take place today, over a period of time, or at some point in the future. Simplicity or complexity can be designed into a planned gift. The gift can take place and have an effect during life, at death, or after death for any period of time or any combination of the above that can be developed.

A planned gift is usually effected to benefit a charitable organization in which the donor has an interest or involvement. That is its intended purpose. The ancillary benefits that accrue to the donor from such a gift can be quite substantial. In addition to the positive emotional and psychological benefits, the monetary consequences to the donor can also be significant. One obvious benefit is a reduction of taxes due to the deductibility characteristics of the planned gift. More significant, however, there can be dramatic increases in current and future income to guarantee more secure retirement years. This can be accomplished through the sale of the trust asset and the reinvestment of the proceeds in a higher-yielding investment.

Many outright gifts can be classified as planned gifts. These type of gifts can take a variety of forms. The most popular type of outright gift is cash. This represents the simplest and easiest form of gift to the charity. A gift is considered made when it is mailed or delivered by hand. For those taxpayers who can itemize deductions, the gift of cash can be deducted in an amount up to 50 percent of adjusted gross income.[9] Thus, the actual cost of a gift is reduced by the amount of tax savings. This added advantage for charitable giving can be an effective incentive to complete a gift by a certain tax deadline.

Gifts of Appreciated Property

The most utilized alternative to gifts of cash are gifts of appreciated assets. This category of assets can offer interesting tax incentives to the donor. The types of appreciated assets that can be given away fall into three general categories: securities, real estate, and tangible personal property.

Gifts of appreciated property, except tangible personal property, can generally be deducted from income at their full appreciated value, not just the cost basis. This rule applies solely to long-term capital gain property. Ordinary income and short-term capital gain property can only be deducted at the original cost basis.

Gifts of Securities

Unlike cash gifts, which can be deducted from ordinary income up to 50 percent of adjusted gross income, gifts of appreciated securities being deducted for current market value can only be utilized on a deductible basis up to 30 percent of adjusted gross income.[10] If the deduction is based upon cost basis rather than current fair market value, an amount up to 50 percent of adjusted gross income may be utilized.[11]

Gifts of Real Estate

Many times, the gift of choice to a charitable organization may be real estate. As with other types of assets, real property has a set of unique issues that the donor must recognize before the gift is made. These issues may entail such questions as ongoing maintenance expenditures, mortgages, major renovation requirements, zoning, or environmental questions. Another issue may be the resale potential. Many charitable organizations are reluctant to assume the responsibilities of property ownership or of being a landlord.

Nevertheless, real estate is a viable charitable vehicle for donors. The same tax treatment that pertains to other types of appreciated assets is applicable to real estate.[12] Both depreciation deducted in prior tax years and leveraged property can present interesting tax questions to the donor. Past deductible appreciation may be brought forward into the current tax year. The gift of leveraged property may result in a taxable event due to the regulations regarding forgiveness of debt.[13] Most of the time, the gift of leveraged property should be viewed with a cautious eye.

Gifts of real estate also require an expert appraisal to determine fair market value.[14] Some ordinary income-type property, as mentioned above, can create a number of complicated tax situations. If the outright sale of the property would have resulted in a taxable ordinary income situation, the gift of the property will force a reduction in the amount of the charitable gift. Therefore, each proposed transaction must be carefully screened.

Gifts of Tangible Personal Property

As with gifts of long-term capital gains securities or real estate, a donor is entitled to a charitable deduction for gifts of long-term capital gain tangible personal property. These assets can be works of art, antiques, rare books, stamp or coin collections, and so on. The tax code provides for certain restrictions on the deductions of most type of assets in this general category. The extent of the deduction for a gift of tangible personal property is dependent on the standard of related use. The standard is relatively clear, but its application can sometimes be confusing.[15]

If the use of the contributed property is related to the exempt purpose of the charity (e.g., a sculpture being donated to a museum), the individual donor is entitled to a charitable deduction. This deduction can be as high as the fair market value of the property. The percentage allowable for use as a deduction for this type of property is the same as for any other long-term capital gain asset, at 30 percent of adjusted gross income, which is the annual limitation. If this one-time deduction cannot be used in the current tax year, it will be available for a five-year carryover.

If the exempt purpose of the charity has no relation to the use of the tangible personal property (e.g., a sculpture to an international relief organization), the deduction amount is limited to the cost basis subject to an annual 50 percent of the adjusted gross income limitation. When the donor is the creator and contributor of the tangible property, the deduction is limited to the actual cost of producing the asset.

The Internal Revenue Service requires, as a general rule, qualified appraisals on all charitable contributions, other than publicly traded securities, where the amount exceeds $5,000. Certain more stringent appraisal reporting requirements apply to gifts valued over $20,000.[16]

INCOME-PRODUCING GIFTS

A number of charitable gifts can be classified as income-producing or split-interest gifts. They can benefit both the donor and the donee. These are summarized in the following categories:

1. Pooled income funds.
2. Charitable gift annuities.
3. Charitable lead trusts.
4. Personal residence charitable remainder trusts.
5. Charitable remainder trusts.

Pooled Income Funds

The pooled income fund by definition is just that—a pool of funds that produce income for the donors. This pool is arranged in a trust by the charitable entity. This entity must be a public charity,[17] also known in the IRS tax code as a 50 percent type charitable organization.

The donor participates in a pooled income fund by irrevocably transferring property to the public charity that has created such a fund. The contribution is then commingled by the fund with other contributions from other donors and invested to produce income. The income earned by the fund each year is paid out to the contributors based upon their individual shares of the pool. At the death of the donor and/or spouse, the remaining assets of his or her share are transferred to the sponsor of the public charity.

The fund cannot invest in any tax-exempt vehicles. The donor must receive, as taxable income, all the income generated each year. The investment decisions are in the hands of the trustees of the fund. No individual donor has any influence or control over the investment decisions.

The donor's inability to select other than a public charity as the remainderman, the recipient of the fund at death, and the inability to influence investment decisions can discourage potential contributors from joining a pooled income fund.

Charitable Gift Annuities

The charitable gift annuity is another popular form of income-producing charitable giving. It is one of the oldest and simplest forms of creating a deferred gift. The donor gives either cash or property to a charitable organization in exchange for a commitment by the organization to provide an annuity income for the duration of the donor's life.

The value of the property transferred to the charitable organization will exceed the value of the annuity income to the donor. The differential is regarded as a charitable gift to the organization.

The committee on gift annuities—a representative body of the philanthropic community recommends rates of payments to be used on gifts to charitable gift annuities. These rates are usually quoted based upon the dollar gift of the donor rather than the actual cost of a dollar of annuity income. The rates are quoted on a unisex basis and are based upon tables provided by the Internal Revenue Service. Interest rates used in these tables vary from 2.2 percent to 26 percent.[18] The rates can vary monthly and are used to value the charitable gift for income tax deduction purposes.

Gifts of cash to charitable gift annuities result in the income received being taxed under the annuity cost-to-recovery rules. Simply stated, a portion of each annuity payment received will be treated as a recovery of cost; the balance of the annuity payment will be treated as taxable income.

A gift of appreciated property to a charitable gift annuity can create a different tax climate. The gift of an appreciated asset for less than its fair market value can create a bargain sale under IRS rules.[19] As such, the gift could result in a part sale, part gift transaction. The tax character of each gift of appreciated property to a charitable organization in exchange for a gift annuity should be thoroughly analyzed before being finalized.

A charitable gift annuity can take two basic forms: an immediate annuity and a deferred annuity. By far, the most popular is an immediate gift annuity. The tax consequences of either type are essentially the same.

Charitable Lead Trusts

The charitable lead trust is different from other forms of planned giving. In fact, it is the opposite of any type of planned income trust. In the charitable lead trust, the charitable organization receives the income, and the donor or a family member usually receives the remainder interest at the end of the trust period. The income stream to the charitable organization can be for a specified period of years or over the life of the individual donor or spouse.[20]

The charitable lead trust is known by various names and comes in three major varieties, the charitable lead annuity trust, the charitable lead unitrust, and the charitable lead income trust. Both the charitable lead annuity trust and unitrust pay a specified percentage to the charity each year.[21] The percentage is paid regardless of the earnings of the trust. Therefore, if earnings are insufficient to make the required payment, part of the principal must be included in the payment. The charitable lead annuity trust pays a specified equal amount each payment. The charitable lead unitrust dispenses a specified percentage of the trust assets each period.

Both of these trusts can be established either while the donor is alive or at the time of death. Either the gift tax or an estate tax charitable deduction is developed at the time of the gift. A lifetime gift could develop an income tax deduction, but this is dependent upon each individual's situation. As an income tax deduction is not a motivating factor with these types of gifts, the most common usage is to create interfamily or intergenerational transfers of property at significant gift or estate tax savings. Care has to be exercised in the use of these vehicles in light of the generation-skipping tax that affects both gifts and estate transfers.

The other type of charitable lead trust is the charitable income trust.[22] In this arrangement, the charitable organization is entitled only to the income earned by the trust. No invasion of principal to make up for an income deficiency is permitted or required, as according to the definition of the trust there are no income deficiencies. There are two varieties of this type of trust: One is used primarily as a vehicle to facilitate interfamily or intergenerational transfers of assets. This type of trust provides for an income gift that is incomplete each year until the donor names a charitable organization as recipient. This results in a gift of income rather than a gift of income interest. At the creation of the trusts, no income, gift, or estate tax deduction is allowed for the donor. The annual income is excluded from the donor's income.

The primary use of this type of lead trust is to pass property to other family members and reduce the values. It can also be used in certain circumstances by the donors who want to accomplish these types of transfers and who currently are substantial givers to charitable organizations. As the income donation to the charity is not a current income tax deduction but does offset the income earned, income in essence has no effect on the maximum allowable charitable income tax deduction. Again, this use has limited application.

There is one final type of charitable income trust that is very rarely used. Here, the donor gives an irrevocable income interest to the charitable organization. Under current law, this creates either a gift tax or estate tax liability to the donor at its inception. Because of this, it is not generally used today.

In summary, the charitable lead trust can be an effective vehicle for either interfamily or intergenerational transfers of property. Much care should be exercised in the application of these trusts in order to assure that the intended results are realized.

Personal Residence Charitable Remainder Trusts

The charitable gift of a remainder interest in a personal residence or farm can provide the donor with a significant current income tax deduction, normally without a noticeable disruption in lifestyle.[23]

In this type of charitable trust, the donor irrevocably transfers to a charitable organization the remainder value in a personal residence or farm. The donor and the donor's spouse, if any, retain a life interest in the property. A current income tax deduction is made available for the remainder value of the property at the end of the life of the donor or the surviving spouse. The charitable organization receives the property at the death of the donor or of the donor's surviving spouse. It is this future transfer at death that entitles the donor to a current income tax deduction.

When the donor guarantees a life estate for other family members or a future generation, the transaction can become very involved, and the current income tax deduction is lost. Some methodologies might work in these scenarios, but each situation requires close scrutiny.

This technique of planned giving has become increasingly popular as many charitable organizations, especially those involved in conservation and land preservation, have promoted the idea. Like any planned gift, proper attention to the individual situation and its unique details can effectuate a beneficial transaction for all involved parties.

Charitable Remainder Trusts

The most discussed and utilized trust vehicle in the income-producing gift area is the charitable remainder trust.[24] Very few trust asset arrangements in recent memory have created such a stir. Naturally, when interest is generated, confusion is also created. There are many misconceptions regarding the proper expectations and use of this planning tool.

During the mid-80s, there was a belief in the advisor and consultant community that donors would be lining up at their doorsteps to install charitable remainder trusts. This belief has not materialized in spite of the tax advantages of the trust and its ability to address the investment dilemma of locked-in profit or gains. Significant numbers of trusts have not occurred, primarily because of the advisors' lack of understanding about donors' motivation for establishing planned gifts.

In a typical charitable remainder trust, the donor irrevocably transfers an asset into the trust and obtains a current income tax deduction for the remainder interest, which will pass to the charitable organization at the end of the trust period. Within prescribed limits, the donor has the ability to determine the amount of income to be distributed to the income recipients (e.g., income of at least 5 percent) to whom it is to be paid, the duration of the payments (e.g., if term of years, duration no longer than 20 years), and the charitable organization that will receive the remainder interest.

The classic asset for use in a charitable remainder trust is one that is highly appreciated—with a low original cost basis—with a high current market value. Publicly traded securities are one of the first types of assets to come to mind. A closely held business that was started on a shoestring and is now significantly increasing in value may be another one. Real estate that has grown in value well beyond its acquisition price is certainly another viable asset for this type of trust. These are just a few examples. The list of these assets is very long.

The major appeal from the conceptual and numerical standpoint of the charitable remainder trust is the fact that as a tax-exempt entity, the trust can sell highly appreciated assets and not recognize capital gains or income tax consequences. With no depletion of the asset value with capital gains or income taxes, the full amount realized upon sale of the asset can be reinvested for the benefit of the income beneficiaries and the charitable organization.

As the trust is a tax-exempt vehicle, the reinvestment occurs in a nontax climate. Future accumulations and income are not diluted at the trust level by income taxes. In most instances, trust dispersal proceeds are taxed to the income recipient. There are some exceptions to full taxation involving return of the principal and tax-exempt income.

For many donors, the ability to free the locked-in profits or gains in assets that have been held for a period of time is a strong motivator. However, practical experience quickly teaches that this economic advantage versus a traditional taxable sale of the asset is often not the ultimate motivating factor that produces a new charitable trust.

To qualify for the charitable deduction for federal estate tax purposes, the income-producing plan must conform to the requirements of either one of the two types of trusts: a charitable remainder annuity trust or a charitable remainder unitrust.

A charitable remainder annuity trust (CRAT) pays out to the income recipient, usually the donor and spouse, a specified income on a periodic basis, at least annually.[25] This income is a fixed amount for the term of the trust. If the earnings of the assets within the trust are not sufficient to produce the desired income, the required balance of the income distribution must be obtained from the principal of the trust. This payment is based on a percentage of the original contribution and is determined at the outset of the trust. This payment can never vary. No additional deposits can be made to an annuity trust once it is established. If subsequent deposits are desired, a new trust must be established each time.

The required distribution from an annuity trust must be a sum certain of not less than 5 percent of the initial fair market value of the assets contributed into the trust.[26] This amount must be paid out at least annually for the term of the trust. If the term of the trust is for a specific number of years, it cannot exceed 20. Normally, the term is the lifetime of the donor or the donor and spouse.

Another test that must be satisfied in a CRAT, is the 5 percent probability test. This stems from an IRS ruling in 1977[27] that disallowed a charitable deduction to an estate for the establishment of a CRAT because the possibility existed due to the terms of the trust that an income beneficiary had more than a 5 percent probability of outliving the funds available.[28] The IRS lost a court case on this particular situation; but the ruling still stands, and prudence dictates designing a trust that complies with this test.

The CRAT is used primarily in those situations where fixed income is desired by the income beneficiary. The reasons for providing a fixed dollar income vary from situation to situation. One common theme, however, can be identified. The shorter the life expectancy, the older the donor and income beneficiary are, and the more important a fixed income stream will become.

The other type of charitable remainder trust is the charitable remainder unitrust (CRUT).[29] Although the differences between the annuity and the unitrust may appear minor, the results can vary significantly. The basic differential is in the methodology of calculating the payments to the income beneficiary. The minimum 5 percent test is similar, but the 5 percent probability test does not apply, as unitrust assets cannot be totally dissipated because the payments are based on the fair market value of the trust's assets, determined annually.[30]

The major difference in calculating benefits to the income recipients revolves around valuation. An annuity trust is valued based upon the initial deposit. A unitrust is valued based upon the fair market value of the trust assets on the annual valuation date. The income payments from a unitrust can therefore fluctuate. Another major difference between the annuity trust and the unitrust is from the contribution standpoint. A CRUT is open-ended. Any number of additional contributions can be made to a unitrust. If and when another contribution is desired, there is no need to draw up a new trust. There may be other reasons, however, for doing so, other than need generated by the desire to make additional deposits.

Unlike the annuity trust, where only one type of trust is available, unitrusts are divided into three categories: the standard unitrust, the net income unitrust, and the net income with makeup unitrust.

The standard unitrust (CRUT) is designed to pay out to the income beneficiary a fixed percentage of the trust assets each year. The percentage is irrevocably set in the trust document and cannot be changed. It must be at least 5 percent annually. If the trust income (dividends and interest) is insufficient to fully fund the required dispersal, the trust principal must be invaded to provide the needed dollars for payment.[31]

The net income unitrust (NICRUT) provides only that income up to an initially selected percentage at the time of trust establishment can be paid out to the income beneficiary. If there is more annual net income produced by the trust asset than is needed for distribution, the net income is added to trust assets for next year's valuation. If net income earned is less than the required percentage amount, the difference between these two cannot be paid out and is permanently lost for payout purposes. If there is no earned income, no payment can be made to income beneficiaries in that year.[32]

The net income with makeup unitrust (NIMCRUT) operates the same way as the NICRUT with one exception. In years where the earnings of the trust assets are less than the stipulated income percentage payout, the deficiency can be accumulated and paid out in later years when the earnings of the trust assets exceed the specified percentage. In either type of net income unitrust, no invasion of principal is permitted.[33]

In evaluating the type of charitable remainder trust to select, all relevant factors must be considered, including the donor's age; if married, the spouse's age; the desired income percentage; the term of the trust; the type of asset being donated; the proposed charitable remainderman, who will act as the trustee or trustees; the donor's investment philosophy, should a replacement of the donated asset occur to the heirs; and, most importantly, the desired outcome.

Probably, the most important item is the last: the desired outcome. What were the donor's objectives when the gift was instituted? What are the desired results? Without these questions being addressed, the satisfaction of the parties involved may be significantly reduced and create unpleasant situations that could have been avoided.

Chapter Three

The Gift Process

THE IDEAL CANDIDATE PROFILE

The ideal candidate for a charitable remainder trust is someone who is charitably minded and who owns a highly appreciated, long-term capital gain asset that is low in yield and readily marketable. This ideal candidate also desires to either increase yield on the asset or convert it into some other investment. This candidate will not sell the asset because of the capital gains tax. This individual also is a modest contributor to charity and is familiar with the charitable income tax deduction.

There are a number of candidates who can be described in this way. Unfortunately, the vast majority of potential donors do not fall into this category. The more common candidate may have the type of asset described but lacks the charitable motivation. This situation is easier to address than the individual who has the charitable motivation but lacks the proper assets. In searching for the ideal candidate, those who possess both the assets and the motivation are often encountered. What prevents them from acting is a lack of understanding of these available charitable trust vehicles or actual, created, or perceived complexity.

Donor Advisors

Any one of a number of individuals or advisors can add complexity to a charitable donation situation. These advisors can come from a variety of sources, such as the individual's family, friends, or business associates. The ideal way to address the complexity issue is for one of the potential donor's advisors to assume the role of coordinator. This is the person who acts as facilitator and assists each member of the advisory team in getting their part done. This facilitator will ease any burden that might be transferred to the donor by any one, individual advisor. The coordinator's goal is to always keep the end objective in mind and not let any of the other advisors lose sight of it.

Advisors come from a variety of disciplines. Among these are philanthropy, accounting, law, investment, insurance, banking, and finance. Quite often, the donor's relatives or friends have an impact on the decision-making process. Any of these individuals can add complexity to the gift-creation process, and unfortunately quite often they do. Often, the key role of the coordinating advisor is critical to the completion of the gift. Let's examine the various approaches of the different advisory groups to a potential donor.

Philanthropic Advisors

The philanthropic community approaches the potential charitable remainder trust donor from the viewpoint of the gift itself, that is, a transaction that will produce a donation or benefit to the organization. They do not as often address the charitable remainder trust as a methodology for dealing with a financial issue that a potential donor currently has or may have in the future. This traditional approach is slowly starting to change.

Legal and Financial Advisors

The legal and financial community, on the other hand, quite often approaches the charitable remainder trust exactly that way—as a vehicle that can address a financial situation for the client, while at the same time satisfying the client's charitable motivation. Often, it is when the legal or financial advisor overemphasizes the financial aspects of the transaction and downplays the charitable motivations that the transaction becomes unraveled and the gift is not completed. The challenge for the advisor is to meld the approaches of these two groups to facilitate the gift.

What types of financial situations would motivate a donor or an advisor to utilize a charitable remainder trust as a possible solution? There are literally dozens of situations. Here is a starter list.

1. The classic case is where an individual owns a highly appreciated asset and is reluctant to sell because of the large capital gains tax.

2. A widow or widower is living on a fixed income, and a significant part of the income is derived from stock dividends. Dividends on this typical (listed) stock range from 2 percent to 2.5 percent. Potential capital gains taxes are also an issue.

3. An investment portfolio consists, to a large degree, of one stock position that has had or could potentially have a large fluctuation in price. Disposing of it by sale and diversifying the portfolio is currently curtailed by the capital gains tax.

4. A sale of a particular asset is desired, but the tax situation creates an impediment. The creation of a program that facilitates a part sale and part charitable remainder trust with the resultant charitable income tax deduction can provide added assistance in making the final numbers more palatable.

5. In order to facilitate an interfamily transfer of a business and maximize the benefits to the sellers, a transfer of the business to a charitable remainder trust must first be facilitated before the subsequent sale from the trust to the desired family members can be accomplished. This can minimize the transfer tax consequences.

6. An individual or a couple has a disabled child. They want to guarantee an income stream after their deaths for care of the child and at the same time make a donation to the organization providing the care. The transfer of an asset into a charitable remainder trust with income payable to the donor and at death payable to the successive income beneficiary, with ultimate distribution of the trust to the charitable organization, would accomplish this objective.

7. A similar situation could be where a donor wishes to guarantee a certain income level to him- or herself, with the asset generating this income protected from creditors. This could prove useful in the event, for example, that the donor is institutionalized for a long illness or because of an age-related infirmity.

8. Quite often, the sale of a closely held business will not be to a family member. The sale could be to the employees or to an

outside party. The charitable remainder trust used in conjunction with other legal instruments, such as employee stock ownership plans (ESOP), can greatly enhance the benefits of the transactions to the donor, at the same time effecting a significant charitable gift.

9. With the restrictions imposed on retirement plans by changes in the Internal Revenue codes, supplemental means of complementing retirement accumulations may be desirous. The tax-free accumulation characteristics of the charitable remainder trust can prove very beneficial in this regard.

10. Estate planning opportunities can also be created by the proper combination of charitable remainder trusts, wills, marital trusts, and life insurance trusts. These combinations can help significantly reduce or totally eliminate estate taxes.

In the development of any of these situations and the many others that can be devised, the charitable intent of the donor must be neither negated nor forgotten. If this is not emphasized, a tremendous amount of effort may be wasted. Quite often, if the emphasis shifts from the donor's intent, the transaction may never be completed and the gift never made. Let's review a typical situation and follow the steps necessary to effect a charitable remainder trust.

TOM AND MARY STEWART

Data Gathering Phase

Tom and Mary Stewart are 64 and 60, respectfully. They have been married for over 25 years and have three children: Jane, 26; Tim, 25; and Brian, 21. Tom owns his own real estate business and employs seven people. Tom and Mary have both worked very hard in the family business and want to start to slow down. In fact, they hope to start turning over the day-to-day operation of the business to Jane, their oldest child, who has worked with them since graduating from college. In addition to their business, their largest single asset is a stock portfolio that Mary inherited from her mother 10 years ago.

TABLE 3–1
Balance of Assets

Type	Amount
Residence	$400,000
Business	$750,000
Real estate	$500,000
Vacation home	$300,000
Investments	$1,000,000
IRA	$1,450,000
Life insurance	$500,000
Total assets	$6,900,000
(Including $2,000,000 stock portfolio)	

Mary's portfolio consists primarily of the stock her deceased father acquired during his working career. Mary inherited the stock at a value of $400,000; it is currently worth $2,000,000. None of the original inheritance has been sold as Mary feels quite possessive of this stock because a great deal of it came from the company where her father spent the majority of his working career. The stock also has an annual yield of 2.25 percent. Tom has been trying to get Mary to sell some of the stock and invest the proceeds into other types of assets. She has been reluctant to do so because of the emotional attachment to the stock and the sizable capital gains tax that will be due on the transaction. The balance of their assets appear in Table 3–1.

As Tom and Mary begin to slow down their day-to-day business involvement, they want to start traveling. Tom's annual earned income has averaged almost $300,000 over the last five years; but with him no longer very active in the business, it will surely diminish. Tom wants to generate sufficient income from their assets so that they can maintain their lifestyle and travel extensively. They consult their financial advisor about what steps to take. There certainly would be enough income if they decided to start taking annual distributions from Tom's IRA, but the Stewarts want to save this as their nest egg until they are in their 70s and forced to take distributions from it.

Initial Planning Phase

Another consideration involves the children. If Jane is ultimately going to end up with the family business, Mary is very insistent that Tim and Brian have the same amount of assets available to them from her and Tom's estate before the commencement of any other division of property. The advisor suggests they reallocate a large portion of their personal investments into income-producing assets and diversify away from the stocks in which they are currently invested. In order to stretch out the impact of the capital gains tax, they agree to adopt this strategy over the next few years. The advisor also suggests the same strategy on the assets Mary inherited from her mother.

After a series of meetings, Mary cannot be persuaded to adopt this strategy on her inherited portfolio. Not only is the large potential capital gains tax dissuading her, but the emotional attachment to the stocks is a major issue. Nothing seems to motivate Mary to initiate any sales in this portfolio. If necessary, the income issue can be solved with the use of the IRA money instead of Mary's inheritance, but another concern regarding Mary's portfolio is raised by the advisor. Mary's stocks have done very well, but over 80 percent of the stock is concentrated in one company, her father's old employer. It has appreciated very nicely but now appears to be running out of steam.

After repeated attempts, the advisor cannot devise a strategy that satisfies Mary' s concerns. Tom is becoming increasingly frustrated with the situation and is ready to agree to start a withdrawal program with the IRA. In one discussion with Mary, the subject arose of her mother's use of the income from the stocks while she was alive. It seems that she was deeply committed to helping her church revitalize the congregation and increase attendance at services. In that light, she was instrumental in raising funds to attract a new progressive minister and to increase the involvement of families in the community. After her mother's death, Mary had carried on her work. She had even taken her mother's place on various church committees.

Social Capital Planning Phase

The advisor had reviewed Mary and Tom's income tax planning in light of their expressed income desires. He had not spent much time on any estate tax planning. He decided to try approaching the situation not from the standpoint of income planning alone, but from a strategic financial planning approach. He called a subsequent meeting with the Stewarts to review their overall planning. The conversation centered around the family's life and involvement in the community for over two generations. The advisor also adopted a social capital approach in his presentation. Here he stressed that no matter what strategy Mary employed with the inherited assets, whether she kept them until death, gave them to her children, or sold them immediately, the total depletion due to taxes would be around 50 percent. Mary's understanding of these tax implications was essential to moving the situation forward.

Finally, the social capital combined with her sense of community involvement with the church stirs a deep interest within Mary. She becomes very animated and talkative. Tom is also starting to get excited, as he saw Mary getting very interested and involved in the process for the first time in these discussions.

Mary has not totally changed her outlook, but she has become an active participant in the ongoing discussions. The advisor, through exploring the use of the social capital concept of voluntary and involuntary philanthropy, had peaked Mary's interest.

Let us revisit the social capital approach to this situation. The Stewarts, especially Mary, have a very strong aversion to paying taxes. By adding estate taxes to the discussion, the advisor was able to heighten this concern. Tom had a vague idea of the impact of estate taxes on their assets, but Mary was pretty much in the dark. When they saw the total tax figure was between $3,000,000 and $4,000,000, they were absolutely shocked. When the advisor was able to demonstrate that a significant part of Mary's mother's legacy was going to the government and not to her children and that she and Tom were the only ones who could do something about it, Mary was much more than interested.

In developing the final recommendations, the advisor kept Mary involved. He described in great detail the interdependence of proper planning and the absolute need for coordination among all the advisory parties. The discussions with Mary and Tom centered around their expressed desire to increase income and Mary's particular objective to preserve her mother's legacy and pass that on to the children as nearly intact as possible. In order to address as many of these goals in the least complicated, most tax-efficient manner, the advisor introduced the concept of a charitable remainder trust. Before doing this, however, one other piece of the planning process had to be more fully explored. This information involved the relationship both Mary and her mother had with the family's church. Without the advisor developing a real charitable purpose and intent, the discussion of the charitable remainder trust would have ended up at a dead end.

As he discussed this relationship with Mary, the advisor tried to solicit if there was any involvement with the church by the Stewarts' children. This proved to be a worthwhile discussion, as Mary noted that Jane currently sang in the church choir, and Brian and his wife taught a class at Sunday school. This revelation helped the advisor develop a theme of family continuity and purpose.

Mary's family, it turned out, had been involved with the church for four generations. The advisor discovered that her grandfather actually helped construct the church with other men in the community. So what he had uncovered was a central family intergenerational theme to further pursue and develop. With this information, along with the other data he had gathered, the advisor was able to solidify the family continuity theme in Mary's mind. He did this by taking the concept of social capital and weaving the data Mary and Tom provided into a cohesive plan that addressed the majority of their objectives, concerns, and interests, even though they had not expressed a number of these issues when they started the planning process with the advisor.

Let us recap how Mary and Tom now feel about the developing plan. The originally stated goal was to develop a methodology that would have a positive impact on improving their current and future income while addressing their fear of excessive taxation on conversion of the assets into more income-orientated ones; to guarantee, as much as possible, the continuance of the same lifestyle in retirement; to slowly ease their way out of the family business and transfer it to their oldest child; and to equalize their estate assets with their other two children.

During the initial data-gathering meetings, at no time was the main objective—Mary's deep unexpressed desire to honor the memory of her parents—really brought to the surface and tied into the rest of the overall planning. If this had been done early on in the interview stage, the number of meetings required to fully expound the entire plan would have been dramatically reduced.

Implementation Phase

The Stewarts' advisor now begins the implementation phase of the planning process. This phase of the plan is equally, if not more, important than the data-gathering and planning phases. It is in this part of many plans that quite a bit of charitable trust planning deteriorates and is never completed. A team of advisors is necessary to complete the process. An ideal advisory team would consist of the following: the accountant, the attorney, the charitable gift administrative consultant, the charitable organization representative, the investment manager, and the life insurance agent.

The vast majority of the time, all of the parties are not involved, and often an advisor may assume more than one role. For a smooth implementation, it is most important that one of the advisors, normally the one who has assembled the team, act as the coordinator. Sometimes this is a difficult assignment due to long-standing advisory roles. Another issue that quite often must be addressed is the many egos involved in this type of arrangement. The role of the coordinator, however, is essential. Without it, the planning process can get mired in conflicting agendas and minute detail. Usually, each client has one advisor that she or he relies upon more than anyone else. This is the one who must be brought into the process early on in order to facilitate a smooth implementation program. If this does not happen early on, at a later date this is the individual who can create the most roadblocks. Probably the number one cause of lack of completion of these programs is this influential advisor's negative reaction to an already determined plan.

Once the entire advisory team is updated and participating, the implementation process can begin. To date, the advisor has not had a detailed discussion with Mary and Tom regarding the amount of the charitable gift, exactly how it is to be arranged, who will be the charitable remainderman, and how much of the principal that is earmarked for the charity will be replaced outside of the estate with a wealth replacement trust. A wealth replacement trust is an irrevocable life insurance trust that is utilized to replace all or a portion of the assets donated into the charitable trust to the heirs. Usually, this topic is brought up much earlier in the discussion process than it has been in the case of the Stewarts. One of the essential steps involves determining the amount of the assets that will be replaced and verifying the availability of the life insurance needed to accomplish this. Verification of insurability normally is done without formal application being made to the insurance company, but in the format of an informal inquiry. It is necessary to use this inquiry approach until all of the needed legal documents are prepared.

By now, a number of computer printouts have been made to illustrate the actual gift, income, and tax deduction numbers. These have been thoroughly reviewed with the Stewarts, their accountant, their lawyer, and their investment advisor. Each of these advisors plays a key role in reviewing the reports and verifying the impact of the implementation of this gift upon the overall planning process. It must be remembered that any of these members of the advisory team could be the initiator of the entire plan and act in the role of coordinator. During this part of the planning process, each advisor is asked to review the plan and verify the conclusions. Any final questions they have raised should be answered at this juncture. Every question or concern has to be addressed and handled. If it cannot be addressed to the satisfaction of the appropriate team member, an acceptable alternative must be found. Any conclusions that are drawn from the review must be disseminated to the other advisors for their comment. This review process does not take place in a vacuum. As in all aspects of this planning process, coordination is the key.

Administration Phase

If it has not been done already, it is essential, at this part of the process, to consult with the organization that is going to be doing the plan administration. The administrator is a key partner in the implementation and ongoing servicing of the charitable trust. Administration can be done by various parties. Often the remainderman charitable organization, if it is large enough in scope, will provide the administrative services. A bank trust department can also provide the necessary administrative services. Another source that has arisen in recent years is the independent administration organization, whose only function is to provide plan administrative services. Depending on the donor's particular situation, any of these resources will work. If the donor wishes to exercise control over the ongoing decision of selecting and supervising the administrative organization, the one that offers the donor the most opportunity for this is the independent firm. This organization is contracted by the donor and serves at the donor's behest. As the firm's only function is to provide trust administrative services, it is operating from a pure administrative viewpoint without any other agendas. This type of firm can be very helpful during the design and installation phase in assisting in developing a plan that can be properly serviced.

It is imperative to once again mention not only the need for coordination among the various advisors, but also the required coordination of documents and the underlying investment vehicles. A donor can become very disillusioned when the executed trust does not provide the required latitude, or investment vehicles do not perform according to trust specifications. An example of this type of problem is a trust that is designed to provide quarterly income distributions, but the investment is in certificates of deposit or in zero coupon bonds. Neither of these types of investment can provide quarterly income distributions, thereby placing the entire trust transaction in jeopardy. Again, coordination is imperative. Another example is a trust that is designed as a net income with makeup unitrust (NIMCRUT). As current income is not the primary objective, the assets should be invested in order to yield little or no current income, but the organization doing the investing pays little heed to the trust design. The investments are made into securities such as high-yielding utility or preferred stocks that create substantial current income, thus defeating the trust design.

While all of this planning and implementation has been going on in the background, what involvement have the Stewarts had in the planning process? Quite a bit. As the computer printouts have been produced, the Stewarts have had to review, with various advisory team members, the feasibility of various plan designs and the impact that each will have on their overall objectives. The narrowing and finalizing of the decision on plan design is now essential.

The Stewarts have now reached the point in the decision process where the final irrevocable decisions have to be made. These involve the amount of the initial contribution that will be put into the trust, the plan design, who will be the income beneficiaries, the payout rate to the income beneficiaries, the term that the trust will run, whether to make the charitable remainderman designation final or subject to substitution of another remainderman, and the timing of the implementation of the trust to coincide with the tax year where the initial deduction is desired. All of the above are irrevocable decisions once the trust is drafted and executed, and the transfer of the asset is made to the trust.

The numerical decisions based upon the computer models are fairly easy to ascertain. It should be remembered that these are also lifestyle decisions. The difference of one percentage point on a lifetime payout rate not only has an impact on the total amount of income received, but on the amount of the current income tax deduction and on the value of the remainder amount for the charitable organization. The relationship is converse: the larger the income percentage, the smaller the tax deduction and vice versa.

There are a few considerations that can affect the lifetime payout rate that are not always quantifiable. These may include such considerations as other sources of income, the current health and the life expectancy of the income beneficiaries, the anticipated impact of inflation on the income stream, the desired charitable remainderman amount, and the anticipated impact upon receipt by the organization. Each of these will affect the decision-making process differently, depending upon the individual situation.

After the Stewarts have made their decisions, the final plan can be selected and given the last review by the advisory team. The trust documents can now be drafted by their attorney. As the attorney has been a member of the advisory team since its inception, this should be a perfunctory procedure. Had the attorney not been involved all along, which under normal circumstances would have been a mistake, this part of the process could take some time, as the attorney's review and drafting is a critical part of the overall planning process. As the trust is an irrevocable one, proper drafting, not only to comply with all the federal and state requirements, but also to accomplish the plan objectives, is essential. A poorly drafted plan can cause significant problems in the operational phase. Often, the incorrect drafting provisions are very difficult, if not impossible, to change.

After considerable thought, Mary and Tom have agreed that they are going to allocate $1,000,000 of the assets that are in Mary's name into the charitable trust. The charitable remainder beneficiary will be their church. Since this will be a charitable remainder unitrust it can, if future circumstances warrant, be supplemented by additional amounts. Now that the amount of the gift has been determined, the Stewarts can review their portfolio to see which of the investments should be earmarked for the gift to the trust. This can be determined in conjunction with the investment counselor who has been their advisor for a number of years.

Mary and Tom also have to decide who will be the trustee of the charitable trust. In most instances, the donor can also act in the role of trustee. In some states, it is necessary to have a co-trustee, along with the donor, who is not an income beneficiary of the trust. In the event of the incapacity or death of the trustee, it is also advisable to name one or more contingent trustees. In the Stewarts' case, they appointed themselves as the trustees and all three children as cotrustees. After the trust has been adopted and the gift of the asset made to the trust, one of the first responsibilities of the trustees is to select the investment manager. The Stewarts elected to stay with the same investment advisor who has handled their investments for a number of years. This investment advisor must now be instructed on how to invest the assets, based upon the desired investment outcome, the trustee's instructions, and the restrictions of the trust.

In conjunction with the legal and investment steps, the Stewarts have also elected to replace the asset gifted to the charitable remainder trust to their children, in the form of a life insurance death benefit. The policy representing this death benefit will be owned outside of the charitable trust in an irrevocable life insurance trust. This will first entail their attorney drafting an irrevocable life insurance trust, naming their three children as the beneficiaries of the trust. Once the trust has been drafted and executed, a formal application will be submitted to the life insurance company for a $1,000,000 survivorship life insurance policy on the lives of Tom and Mary. This policy will be applied for and owned by the irrevocable trust. The trust will also be the beneficiary of the policy. The death benefit of the policy will be paid upon the death of the survivor of Tom and Mary. The Stewarts have previously made an informal inquiry to the insurance company to verify their insurability. The insurance company, based upon an evaluation of their health from information obtained from their doctors, has indicated their preliminary acceptance.

This formal application, along with the required physical examinations, will result in a policy being issued upon their lives. The premium on this policy is to be paid with funds gifted into the irrevocable life insurance trust by the Stewarts. The initial premium dollars given into this trust can come from either the tax savings generated by the charitable remainder trust gift or from current assets or income. In subsequent years, the gifts for premium payments may come from either the unused tax savings from prior years or, if these are unavailable or insufficient, the increased income created by the reinvestment of the charitable trust assets in areas that will produce a higher income stream than is currently being realized. This increased income will be available during the first year but will not be available initially when the trust is established.

Now that the Stewarts have identified the assets to be transferred into the trust and this has been accomplished, the investment advisor can now dispose of the assets based upon the instructions from the trustee. As the charitable trust is a tax-exempt entity, these transactions and all subsequent investment decisions will take place in a tax-free environment. The fact that the investment scenario is a tax-free one, will allow the investment advisor to make decisions designed to enhance the investment's performance, according to trust specifications, without regard to the tax consequences of the transaction.

The other important step for the Stewarts to take in conjunction with the rearrangement of their assets is to have a meeting with their children and the coordinating advisor. One aspect of the gifting process that Tom and Mary did not want to overlook was the further involvement of their children in the Stewarts' church activities.

Tom and Mary wanted their children to fully understand the process they went through in evolving their retirement and estate plan. They also wanted them to realize that the children will be receiving substantial assets at their death and that they could also have, if they wished, ongoing input into the financial activities of their church. Upon telling the minister about their intentions of creating the charitable remainder trust, Tom and Mary had suggested that the church create an endowment committee. The purpose of this committee would be to decide on the annual dispersal of funds from the capital account and to encourage other families within the church to follow the example set by the Stewarts. The minister thought this was a wonderful idea and suggested that one of the Stewarts' children serve as head of this new committee. Tom and Mary concurred on this idea and were delighted to present it to their children. The children also had to be made aware of the balance of the planning that Tom and Mary were doing, as each of them was an income beneficiary of the irrevocable life insurance trust and had a decision to make each year regarding the dispersal of the annual gift made into the trust on his or her behalf.

One significant benefit that occurs in a number of gifting situations with families is the involvement of the next generation in the planning process. Mary was very cognizant of the community pride and concern that was expressed by her parents and grandparents. She and Tom had seen to it that their children, during their formative years, had been involved in community activities. Now, with the charitable remainder trust, they saw a methodology for increasing this involvement in the future and preserving the legacy of Mary's family.

Finalization

The final step in this process is for the Stewarts to meet with their attorney to review their will and be sure that it coordinates with all the recent planning that had taken place. A new will, additional estate planning trusts, and other legal instruments will be prepared. It is also important at this juncture to be sure that their accountant is abreast of all the changes that have been made. The coordinating advisor has to be sure that all the final pieces of the plan are put into place. It is also this individual's role to supervise the annual reviewing process to assure that the total plan keeps pace with any changes in the Stewarts' lifestyle. During the first operational year of the trust, a number of issues will arise that will require the advisor's involvement.

Having now gone through a very detailed and lengthy planning process, what have the Stewarts accomplished? Their originally stated goal was to start to ease into retirement and to replace any earned income lost in this transition with income from their investments. They also wanted to preserve the IRA asset as long as possible, as they regarded these dollars as their safety net. Tom also wanted to find some method of increasing the yield on Mary's stocks.

The advisor, by reviewing the key concept of social capital, conveyed to the Stewarts that they had the ability to dramatically influence the outcome of the total taxes paid on their assets. This could be accomplished while satisfying a deep-seated interest in both of them to assure the future involvement of their children and in turn to carry on a family tradition in their local community. The mechanism that was the cornerstone of this planning process was the charitable remainder trust. The use of this instrument allowed a number of their overall, lifetime objectives to be developed into one coordinated planning process.

By allocating $1,000,000 of Mary's stocks to the charitable trust, the Stewarts removed this asset from their estate. This reduced their overall federal estate tax obligation by $600,000. The stocks, which had built up considerable capital gains, could now be sold by the charitable trust without payment of any capital gains tax. The proceeds from this sale could now be invested into other types of investments, such as corporate bonds, to yield a dramatically increased income stream to the Stewarts. The gift transaction will also create a sizable current income tax deduction, which can be used to reduce the Stewarts' present income tax obligations. By diverting a portion of the tax savings and increased income stream to fund a life insurance policy within an irrevocable life insurance trust, the Stewarts will also provide an estate tax-free source of dollars for their children. These funds could be utilized to buy assets from the estate to provide liquidity to help pay estate taxes. The monies received in the life insurance trust could also be used to help equalize the division of the Stewarts' estate among the three children or for any number of other purposes. While they are revising their will, the Stewarts can also address, if need be, the estate equalization issue.

With the combined concepts of social capital and the charitable remainder trust, the Stewarts were able to develop a coordinated retirement and estate plan. This plan provided them with a great degree of flexibility. They were able to convert a relatively nonproductive asset into one that produced significant income. This was not done in isolation, but in conjunction with an overall planning process. The key that solidified the establishment of the charitable trust was the total planning process. Without the Stewarts' ability to view the charitable gift within their total plan, it might never have been created.

Chapter Four
Income and Estate Tax Considerations

THE HISTORY OF CHARITABLE TRUSTS

The charitable remainder trust was a concept created by Congress with amendments to the Internal Revenue Code in 1969.[1] These amendments also created charitable lead trusts, charitable income trusts, and pooled income funds.[2] Prior to these legislative changes, charitable split interest trusts were nonexistent. It took quite a few years for the charitable remainder trust concept to become an integral part of the income and estate planning of a number of people. Because of the range of mathematical calculations required to illustrate the concept, the use of a computer program proved extremely helpful. But it was not until the 1980s that computer programs were designed to address this illustration problem.

TYPES OF TRUSTS

A charitable remainder trust can be either a living (inter vivos) or a testamentary (at death) trust. The instrument used most frequently is the living trust. Whether the trust is a living or testamentary one, it must satisfy all of the complex rules and requirements imposed by the original Internal Revenue Code statutory language and all subsequent statutory changes. These substantive changes are contained not only in the Internal Revenue Code, but in the rules and regulations. If the trust qualifies under all the statutory and interpretive requirements, it will be eligible for deduction under income, gift, and estate tax regulations.

In the living trust situation, the trust is eligible for an income tax deduction for the present value of the remainder interest that will pass to the charity. At the end of the term of the trust, the remainder is determined by using the appropriate Internal Revenue tables. This remainder interest can also qualify as a charitable gift for federal gift tax deduction purposes. It's essential that the living gift qualify for both deductions. The consequences of not qualifying are loss of the income tax deduction and the loss of the gift tax deduction.

As the qualified remainder interest will be deductible from the estate assets, it will not be included in the estate upon the death of the donor. If the charitable remainder trust is a testamentary one, the deduction for estate tax purposes may be less than the value of the remainder interest. This will depend upon who the testamentary income beneficiary is. If it is someone other than the spouse of the donor, this restrictive deduction limitation will become operable. Each individual situation requires careful review and coordination before a conclusion regarding the tax consequences can be drawn.

Since the passage of the enabling statutes in 1969, there have been numerous regulatory changes. The majority of the changes have been clarifying in nature and not at all repressive. A few years after the initial code sections were implemented, a number of revenue rulings were published containing sample trust language along with appropriate mandatory and suggested sections.[3] These initial language and required sections have now been expanded to encompass a number of complete documents. The Internal Revenue Service has assembled the sample trusts into prototype style documents for use by the donor's legal counsel.

In the majority of cases, for a number of valid reasons, the donor's attorney will want to draft an individual trust document for the donor client and not utilize the prototype document. The Internal Revenue Service has assured the taxpayers that as long as the sample language is closely followed, they will recognize the document as meeting all the requirements. In both the prototype format and the individually drafted scenario, the IRS assumes that the trust will in its operational phase comply with all the requirements of the trust instrument and with the appropriate state laws. Since this program has been operational, the IRS has refrained from issuing private letter rulings to individual taxpayers. In fact, in recent years, the requests for private letter rulings have been systematically discouraged.[4]

INCOME TAX DEDUCTIBILITY

In the living trust situation, the income tax deductibility of the remainder interest often provides an added impetus to the gift transfer. Individual tax scenarios may be addressed with appropriately timed gifts. The deductibility of the remainder interest is important; but the vast percentage of the time, from a purely economic point of view, the value of making the gift will still stand even without a current income tax deduction. In most instances involving gifts of appreciated assets, the ability to avoid the capital gains tax is of sufficient economic worth to justify the gift. The mere fact that the entire principal amount will remain intact to produce income for the beneficiaries in comparison to the sale of an asset depleted by a large capital gains tax can often justify the charitable gift.

For an individual taxpayer, the maximum allowable annual deduction is 50 percent of the taxpayer's contribution base. The contribution base is the adjusted gross income without regard to any net operating loss. Before the individual can calculate the charitable gift income tax deduction, a few other issues must be considered. Initially, the tax status of the charitable organization must first be determined. In order for the gift to be eligible for the maximum deductibility category, the organization must be one that qualifies under the Internal Revenue Code.[5] Basically, qualified organizations are those that are operated exclusively for religious, educational, medical or hospital care, a governmental unit, and certain types of private foundations. Any charitable organization that does not qualify as a 50 percent organization is referred to as a 30 percent organization. The IRS publishes a list of all organizations that qualify to receive gifts that are income tax deductible. This publication is commonly referred to as the "Blue Book."[6]

Once the tax status of the organization has been established, the next step is to determine the percentage limitation of the individual gift. The types of property that qualify for the maximum 50 percent of the contribution base deduction are cash, like-kind cash assets, and any other assets that are not long-term capital gain property. Any property whose sale would constitute a short-term capital gain or yield an ordinary income tax would qualify in this category. Any long-term capital gain property whose charitable gift deduction was calculated on the acquisition basis, not on the appreciated value, would also qualify under the 50 percent limitation.

LONG-TERM CAPITAL GAIN PROPERTY

All long-term capital gain property where the charitable gift deduction is based upon the appreciated value is classified in a 30 percent of contribution base deduction category. This limitation on long-term appreciated capital gain property pertains to the individual gift, even though the charitable recipient is a 50 percent organization. If the charitable recipient is a 30 percent organization, the long-term appreciated property deduction is limited to 20 percent of the contribution base. Additional limitations on the actual amount that is deductible in a given tax year on long-term capital gain appreciated property may also be due to the required deductibility calculation formulas for years in which there are also additional deductible contributions of 50 percent type property.

In certain instances, it may prove advantageous based upon the total charitable deduction available to calculate the long-term capital gain gift on the acquisition basis: the basis less the value of the long-term capital gain that would have been received had the property been sold. If this calculation method is utilized, the deduction can be up to 50 percent rather than 30 percent of the contribution base.[7] Depending on the total individual tax picture, this method may work out quite favorably.

Quite a number of issues can affect the actual charitable gift deduction when long-term capital gain property is the funding vehicle. One example that can cause unintended results is where the gifted property has been subject to an accelerated depreciation schedule for income tax deduction purposes. The accelerated depreciation must be recaptured by the donor for income tax purposes as ordinary income in the year of the gift.

Another example is the gift of long-term capital gain property that is encumbered or mortgaged. The amount of the gift must be reduced by the debt, plus this type of gift will create other adverse income tax consequences. Each individual situation has to be judged on its own merits, but basically this type of transaction falls under the auspices of the "bargain sale" rules.[8] This particular set of rules will result in virtually all charitable remainder trust gift transactions taxable to the donor for all or a significant portion of the forgiven debt. It is always advisable to be extremely careful in utilizing mortgaged property for charitable remainder trust donations. In fact, a good rule of thumb is to avoid the use of mortgaged property entirely.

A third and final example of the issues that can be encountered in donating an asset to a charitable remainder trust is when the gift is made into the trust after some form of understanding has been reached with a potential buyer. In the instance where the donor entered into a letter of intent or a binder of sale prior to the actual gift, a serious tax consequence will result. For example, all of the charitable gift deduction may be lost, the property may be transferred to the charitable trust, and the donor may suffer capital gains or income tax consequences when the charitable trust sells the property. Consequently, each charitable gift situation should be thoroughly reviewed before being finalized.

VALUATION OF SECURITIES

Gifts of property other than cash and cash equivalents are all subject to the rules and regulations regarding valuation. In order to assure the validity of the amount of the gift and the ensuing income tax deduction, proper valuation is essential. For gifts of publicly traded securities, the valuation process is relatively simple. The value to be used for the gift is the mean price between the highest and lowest selling prices on the date of the gift. For example, if a stock traded between $98 and $100 on a given day, the mean price would be $99.[9] If there was no trading activity on that date, a weighted average approach for valuation is used. The weighted average of the mean sale prices on the nearest day before and after the date of the gift is calculated and used as the valuation figure.[10] Listed bonds follow the same valuation strategy as listed stocks.

In some instances, determining the valuation of a listed security can prove troublesome. This can be especially true when there is no activity in that security. The Internal Revenue Service has developed rules and regulations to cover most circumstances. Consulting these regulations and utilizing the methodologies described will provide for proper valuation of the charitable gift.

Mutual fund shares provide for a relatively easy valuation. The value for deduction purposes is the closing redemption price on the date of the gift. If for some reason there was not a published redemption price on the date of the gift, the last closing price available is used as the valuation price.[11]

Valuations of nonlisted securities and closely held stock for charitable gift purposes can pose some interesting problems. To help alleviate these questions, the Internal Revenue Service has outlined a series of steps and procedures to guide the taxpayer and the accounting practitioner in calculating the value of the gift. The most secure method of valuation is to have an appraisal done by a qualified appraiser.

It makes little sense to have the appraisal done by an individual or company whose qualifications or credentials can be questioned. Quite often, a large income tax deduction is created by the charitable gift. Not securing a qualified appraisal could be very detrimental in the event that the IRS challenges the valuation. In the event that the donor decides to forgo hiring a qualified appraiser, the IRS valuation guidelines can be followed by the trustee. This procedure, however, will most likely be more open to tax audit challenge.

HARD-TO-VALUE ASSETS

The majority of the remaining assets not previously discussed fall into the general category of hard-to-value assets. In addition to closely held stock, this category includes such assets as real estate restricted securities, business inventory, fractional interests in property, and personal property, such as art, literary collections, stamp or coin collections, automobiles, boats, jewelry, and antiques. The best way to address the valuation of any type of personal property is by securing a qualified appraisal. In fact, the Internal Revenue Service requires a qualified appraisal on all charitable gifts of property in excess of $5,000.[12]

The basic question from the Internal Revenue Service's point of view with respect to gifts of personal property is whether there has been overvaluation for income tax deduction purposes and undervaluation for other purposes. Such an undervaluation may be desirous in the transfer of the property to other family members. This concern is of such major significance that over 25 years ago the service established a panel of art experts to review taxpayers' appraisals used in support of the deducted charitable contribution. These reviews have resulted in consistent reductions in the amounts used for charitable gift tax deductions. The reviews have also resulted in increases in the valuations of gifts claimed under gift and estate tax transfers. Problems with valuations not only result in changes in the taxes owed, but can result in large penalties being assessed against the taxpayer. Significant penalties can also be imposed upon the charitable organization for failure to file the required informational returns.

TAXATION OF INCOME RECEIVED FROM THE TRUST

The income received by the income recipient of a charitable remainder trust is taxable upon receipt. This applies to both annuity and unitrusts. Both of these types of charitable trusts are entities created by the tax code. They internally operate, exempt from income taxes. The income paid to the income beneficiaries is taxable. The extent to which each payment is taxable, however, depends upon the character of the payment, which is judged under the special income tax calculation formula particular to charitable remainder trusts. The Internal Revenue Code imposes a special four-tier accounting procedure to determine the tax character of the income distribution to the beneficiary. This procedure is unique to charitable remainder trusts.[13]

One of the easiest ways to view this special procedure is to compare it to other accounting rules. There is a good degree of familiarity with the inventory control accounting reporting systems of LIFO—last in, first out and FIFO—first in, first out. In these procedures in accounting for the value of inventory, either the last price paid for the item or the first price paid for it determines the total value of the inventory. A similar concept can be applied to the income tax obligation attributable to payments to the income beneficiaries of charitable remainder trusts.

The acronym to describe the accounting rule is WIFO—worst in, first out. The highest income tax that is currently imposed is on ordinary income. The moneys received are first taxed to the extent of the ordinary income earned within the trust in the current tax year along with any undistributed ordinary income from prior years. If there is still a distribution required after exhausting the ordinary income, it will be taxed at capital gains rates to the extent of the capital gains realized in the current year and any undistributed capital gains from prior years. If there is a need for further distributions, they would be calculated from the tax-exempt income, if any, in the current year or accumulated from prior years. Finally, if a further distribution is required by the trusts, specifications will come from the principal or corpus of the trust.

This accounting procedure is of particular importance for annuity trusts (CRATS) and standard unitrusts (CRUTS). It does not apply to net income unitrusts (NICRUTS) or to net income with makeup unitrusts (NIMCRUTS). This calculation comes to fruition when there is insufficient income either currently earned or accumulated from previous years to satisfy the required trust distribution. In that case, the required percentage must be distributed and a dispersal made to the income beneficiaries. If the trust has already received capital gains, either from the current or prior years, and tax-exempt income is unavailable for distribution, a dispersal must be made from the principal of the trust.

If the donor's contribution to the trust consisted entirely of nonappreciated assets, this distribution will represent a return of principal. If, however, the contribution consisted of appreciated property, the distribution from principal will have an income tax consequence to the recipient beneficiary. This income tax will take the form of a capital gains tax to the extent that any of the distribution is attributable to gains that were untaxed prior to the asset being transferred to the trust. The donated asset therefore carries with it the tax characteristics that existed prior to the actual gift being made to the charitable trust. A previously untaxed capital gain will not be cleansed by merely contributing the asset that contains such a gain to a charitable remainder trust.[14]

This four-tier accounting procedure can present a number of problems for the unwary. One of the initial questions often asked by uninformed donors and advisors who are not familiar with charitable remainder trusts involves the conversion of significantly appreciated assets into municipal bonds with tax-exempt income. This question usually arises after they learn that the income from the charitable remainder trust is taxable to the income beneficiary. Once the appreciated assets are sold within the trust, the trustees can direct investments into various asset categories. Municipal bonds may be a suitable trust investment. The income from the municipal bonds will either be partially or entirely subject to the capital gains tax. The portion taxable will be dependent on whether or not the entire gain has been previously withdrawn.

POMONA COLLEGE PLAN

A few years prior to the introduction of charitable remainder trust legislation, there was a very popular life-income plan (the Pomona College Plan) that was built around the premise of converting appreciated stocks and bonds into tax-exempt bonds. The income generated by the bonds was distributed without any income tax consequences being recognized by the income recipient. Under this plan, the donor contributed appreciated stocks or bonds to a charitable institution. They in turn sold these investments and purchased tax-exempt municipal bonds. Under this arrangement, neither party recognized any tax consequences on the sale. The charitable organization then paid out the tax-exempt interest to the income beneficiary, who did not report it as income.

As this plan became well-known, the Internal Revenue Service invoked new legislation to ban its use. The attendant regulations changed the basic ground rules on this type of transaction and required that the gain be taxable to the donor.[15]

CHARITABLE TRUST ADMINISTRATION

An integral part of this entire process is the ability of the charitable remainder trust administrator to track these transactions both from a historical and current prospective. Each time an asset is sold by the trust and a gain is received, it must be recorded and tracked. Before any nontaxable distributions can be made to the income recipient, all cumulative and current capital gains must be totally reconciled. The trust administrator is the vital link in this tracking process. Without a sophisticated computer tracking system, this task will be daunting. Mistakes made in the reporting process between the trust administrator and the income recipient can cause severe income tax problems for the income recipient. This is one major reason why the selection of a competent trust administrator is paramount.

Whether the income being paid out is from municipal bonds or any other type of investment, when the donated property had as one of its valuation components untaxed capital gains, this issue will be present. Calculating all of the necessary figures requires a very sophisticated tracking system. Without this capability, the trust operation will be in jeopardy.

VALUATION OF INCOME TAX DEDUCTION

Valuing the charitable income tax deduction is an integral part of the charitable remainder trust calculation process. As previously mentioned, many charitable trusts will still be very attractive arrangements even without the current income tax deduction. The income tax deduction makes the whole transaction that much more viable. Prior to the technical and miscellaneous revenue act of 1988 (TAMRA), the calculation required only consulting an IRS table to develop the necessary factor.

This procedure changed dramatically with the introduction of the regulations governing the valuation process. The new rules require that the value of the income of any deferred gift, annuity, life or term of years interest, remainder, or reversion under a charitable remainder trust be calculated by the use of an interest rate that is 120 percent of the federal midterm rate in effect for valuing certain federal government debt instruments for the month of the gift. In addition, the calculation must use as a mortality factor the most recent mortality experience table available.[16] The Internal Revenue has developed publications reflecting these actuarial valuations.[17] If done by hand, these calculations require a number of steps; but with the computer programs available today, they can be done quickly and easily.

VALUATION OF ESTATE AND GIFT TAX DEDUCTION

The estate and gift tax legislation of 1976 created a uniform system of taxation for transfers made as a gift or at death. These regulations, combined with the generation-skipping tax legislation of 1986 and 1988, have created the current transfer tax system. The overall purpose of these rules and regulations is to make it much more difficult to pass assets from one generation to the next without significant transfer costs being interjected by the government. Gift and estate taxes are very high and the generation-skipping transfer tax has all but precluded any transfers to second generation beneficiaries in amounts above the lifetime $1,000,000 exclusion level.

Unique to both the gift and estate tax is the fact that they are not only progressive in nature, but they are also cumulative. During the donor's life, the value of the annual taxable gifts are added to the value of all the taxable gifts made in prior years to determine the rate of tax on the current taxable gift. Once this is calculated and the total tax determined, the taxes paid in prior years are deducted from the total tax figure to arrive at the net tax due for the gifts made during the current year.

Estate taxes are imposed in a manner similar to the gift tax regulations. The estate tax is calculated on all assets owned by the decedent at the time of death. The estate tax calculation, "being both progressive and cumulative in nature requires that all taxable lifetime gifts made after December 31, 1976, be added to the value of the taxable estate to determine the optimum tax rates that will apply to the estate.[18] This is a necessary part of the calculation formula because as of this date the gift and estate tax systems were combined into the current unified transfer tax approach. Once the total tax due on all transfers from this date is determined from the progressive tax tables, any prior gift transfer taxes paid are deducted from the total tax due to arrive at the net tax payable when the estate tax return is filed.

In most cases, the largest single tax to which the assets of the affluent taxpayer are ever going to be exposed is the federal gift and estate tax. Proper estate planning can help to alleviate the tax situation, and charitable gift planning can be an integral part of that overall process.

In contrast to the situation under income taxes regulations, there are no limitations on the deductible amount of the assets that may be given or bequeathed to a charitable organization. Amounts up to the entire estate value may be donated to qualified charitable organizations. It is therefore possible for taxpayers to totally eliminate all gift and estate taxes by donating their entire estate to a qualified charity. For most individuals, however, this is not often a practical estate tax avoidance solution. An alternative is to utilize this unlimited gift tax deduction capability in the context of a charitable remainder trust. This does present some extremely interesting planning opportunities. Because of its unique split-interest gift and income capabilities, the charitable remainder trust is an extremely powerful tool, especially when used in conjunction with other sophisticated estate planning techniques.

THE UNLIMITED MARITAL DEDUCTION

Most individual taxpayers are somewhat familiar with the workings of the unlimited marital deduction. Under the current combined system of gift and estate taxes, the unlimited marital deduction plays a key role in both intermarital transfer situations and delaying the impact of estate taxes. This deduction is available both for lifetime transfers between spouses and for testamentary transfers to the surviving spouse.[19] Many taxpayers are under the false impression that the estate tax is negated in spousal transfers. It is not avoided; it is only delayed. It is important to remember that a number of taxpayers confuse the unlimited marital deduction with the unified credit for the tax on $600,000 of assets owned by each taxpayer.[20] The unified credit is available to each and every taxpayer. The unlimited marital deduction is not, however, available to each and every spouse, but only to spouses who are U.S. citizens.[21] This issue can present interesting estate planning questions to a married couple when one spouse is not a citizen.

Under normal circumstances, qualifying a transfer of a terminable interest to a spouse is not considered deductible under the unlimited marital deduction. A terminable interest is one that ceases at the death or other event, such as a remarriage of the survivor. Thus a remainder interest that passes to another party at the death of the surviving spouse is considered a terminable interest.[22] Therefore, under this rule the income from a charitable remainder trust left to a surviving spouse would not qualify for the marital deduction. In order to compensate for this code section, a special section was added to the Internal Revenue Code that allows for the qualification of a charitable remainder trust for the marital deduction, provided that the surviving spouse is the only other income beneficiary.[23] As the marital deductions for both gift and estate taxes are addressed under the unified rules, the availability of the marital deduction in either a gift or a death situation is the same.

CHARITABLE TRUSTS UTILIZING NONSPOUSAL BENEFICIARIES

The institution of charitable remainder trusts with nonspousal beneficiaries creates a number of gift and estate tax issues. Each taxpayer is permitted to give to any number of individuals a gift of $10,000 on an annual basis without incurring a gift tax on the transaction.[24] Married donors may make joint annual gifts to any number of individuals up to twice this amount by having the gift treated as if each spouse were gifting $10,000.[25] If the income amounts exceed the annual gift tax exclusions, either a gift tax must be paid or a portion of the lifetime $600,000 exemption must be utilized to avoid the taxes due. In order to have the income beneficiary of a charitable remainder trust be someone in addition to or other than the donor or the spouse, the annual gift tax exclusion must come into play. If the annual exclusion is not sufficient to fully satisfy the required gift amount, a portion of the lifetime exclusion must be utilized or a gift tax paid.

If the income beneficiary of a charitable remainder trust is someone in addition to the donor's spouse or another party entirely, the income stream received by the nonspousal beneficiary will be part of the estate of the deceased donor. The part that is in the estate is the present value of the income stream to the nonspousal beneficiary. The income is included in the donor's gross estate under the IRS rules entitled income in respect of a decedent.[26]

GENERATION-SKIPPING TAX TRANSFERS

The last major component of the current transfer tax system is the generation-skipping tax. This is a tax imposed when assets are passed through gift or bequest to a generation at least one generation beyond the next generation.[27] The usual example is that of a grandfather who sets up a trust for his child, with the income from the trust going to the child but the property passing to the grandchild at the death of the child. The transfer would be in the estate of the grandfather for estate tax purposes but not in the estate of the child. Instead, it would be in the estate of the grandchild. The estate tax that would normally have been due on the death of the child had the property been directly left to the child is "skipped," or not collected by the Internal Revenue Service. The estate tax would not be due until the death of the grandchild. To discourage the use of this planning technique, elaborate and complex rules were written into the tax code.

The application of the generation-skipping transfer tax to charitable remainder trusts takes effect when there are income beneficiaries of the trust that are more than one generation removed from the donor. The application of the complex generation-skipping tax rules and the ensuing calculations require careful consideration before adopting this planning technique in charitable remainder trusts.

Because of the irrevocable nature of charitable remainder trusts, careful consideration has to be given to all of the income and estate tax considerations in each and every situation. Each charitable remainder trust is unique unto itself. All donors who create a charitable remainder trust should be well aware of the ramifications of their actions, both to themselves and to all the concerned parties. Irrevocable decisions should not be made without a good deal of forethought.

Chapter Five

Personal Applications—
Individual Utilization

COMMON USES OF CHARITABLE
REMAINDER TRUSTS

The most common use of charitable remainder trusts has been in the gifting of highly appreciated, low-yielding securities to charitable organizations in order to produce a higher stream of income to the donor. A number of other applications of the charitable remainder trust can also be useful to an individual in the correct set of circumstances. When suggesting the use of a charitable remainder trust, it is paramount that all parties involved remember that the strongest overriding psychological motivation to guarantee completion of the gift will be the charitable one.

In considering the conversion of an underperforming asset into one that will provide a desired stream of income, tax impact is always in the forefront. Having an additional 28 percent of the principal available to produce income will have a major impact on the viability of the income stream and quite often the lifestyle of the donor. Let's review the choices that an individual has in the conversion of a low-yielding, highly appreciated security. The approach that will be taken is to observe this transaction from three viewpoints: (1) holding on to the asset until death without any conversion, (2) selling the asset and reinvesting the proceeds at a higher rate of return, and (3) donating the asset to a charitable remainder trust and having the trust sell the asset and reinvest the proceeds into an investment vehicle with a higher rate of return.

TABLE 5–1
Scenario Comparisons

	Hold	Convert	Gift
Asset value	$500,000	$500,000	$500,000
Income tax deduction	0	0	78,505
Capital gains tax	0	166,600	0
Net income for life	334,643	380,823	600,952
Gross estate value	1,849,368	333,400	0
Estate taxes	1,017,152	183,370	0
Net estate	832,215	150,030	0
Endowment to charity	0	0	1,100,952

Source: American Renaissance Trust Information Services, Version 3.01 © 1992
PhilanthroTec, Inc.

The parameters of this example (Table 5–1) are as follows:

Client: Male, age 55 and Female: age 57

Adjusted gross income: $125,000

Marginal federal income tax bracket: 38 percent

Federal Capital gains tax rate: 28 percent

Assumed state capital gains tax rate: 36 percent

Marginal federal estate tax bracket: 55 percent

Total asset values: $4,000,000

Asset value: $500,000

Asset cost basis: $10,000

Current investment annual yield: 2 percent

Current investment annual appreciation: 5 percent

Desired annual investment return: 7 percent

Current deductible charitable gifts: $4,000

Let us examine in detail the outcome of the different arrangements. As the example is reviewed, remember that the overriding financial objective is to increase income. As can be seen from this example, the advantages of a gift to the charitable trust makes strong financial sense. The fact that it also may make strong psychological sense should not be discounted. The objective in the above example was solely to maximize current income. Had the objective been something other than or in addition to this, a different approach could be taken. In this situation, the plan objective has been accomplished.

We can now review what the alternative solutions produced. If these clients had held onto the asset until their death at normal life expectancy, the net annual income would have started at $6,155 and grown to $21,689 at the death of the survivor. This growth in income is based upon the increase in the value of the underlying asset. The growth in the income stream may not materialize unless the growth in dividends keeps pace with the growth in stock value.

In the second approach where the asset is sold for reinvestment purposes, the capital gains tax must first be paid. In the above example, that amounts to $140,000 on the federal level. In addition to the federal capital gains tax, the majority of states impose their own capital gains tax. In the above example, that would bring the total capital gains tax to $166,600. The remaining $333,400 reinvested in corporate bonds at the rate of 7 percent will yield $14,105 on a net after-tax annual basis. This results in an increase in the initial annual net spendable income of $7,950. As increased income is the intended result of the individual, the sale and subsequent reinvestment certainly accomplishes this objective. This is done, however, at the expense of a $166,600 capital gains tax.

In the case of the charitable remainder trust, the same sale of the securities takes place, but it occurs in a tax-exempt environment. The resultant reinvestment of the proceeds of the sale are therefore not depleted by the capital gains tax. The net after-tax annual income in the first year is $21,153. This is an increase in net spendable income of $14,998 from the hold scenario and $7,048 from the convert scenario. Not only is this a significant dollar increase, but it is also a very large percentage increase. The increase from the hold scenario to the gift scenario is a 243 percent increase. The comparison between the convert scenario and the gift scenario is a 50 percent first-year increase in after-tax

TABLE 5–2
Present Value Comparisons

	Hold	Convert	Gift
Net income for life	$146,686	$197,508	$325,309
Net estate	182,929	32,978	0
Total net family value	329,616	230,486	325,309

Source: American Renaissance Trust Information Services, Version 3.01 © 1992 PhilanthroTec, Inc.

spendable dollars. The other advantage of the gift to the charitable trust is the creation of an income tax deduction. The value of the income tax savings at a 38 percent bracket plus the savings in taxes on the capital transfer amounts to $196,432. These are actual dollar savings that will benefit the individual in increased income, both initially and on an annual basis.

One of the interesting comparisons is in the present value calculations of the income stream and the overall value of the transaction to the family. This cumulative total value to the family produces the following net present value comparisons at a 6 percent discount calculation (see Table 5–2).

Note that in the present value figures the increase in cumulative net after-tax spendable dollars represent a 35 percent increase between the hold and convert modules. In the comparison between the hold and gift columns, the net after-tax spendable dollars, the differential increase is 122 percent. That is an increase of three and one-half times, a sizable expansion. The percentage variance between the convert scenario and the gift is a 65 percent gain on behalf of the giving arrangement. This increase in net present value is quite substantial and dramatically illustrates the accomplishment of the stated objective.

The downside of the gift transaction is the loss of the use of the principal. This loss is both current and in the future, in that it can no longer be left to an heir. This is the main reason that, with rare exception, all of the inevitable assets are not put into a charitable trust. In the majority of situations, there are other sufficient assets for use in the event of a family crisis or emergency. In a scenario where there is a desire to pass on to an estate beneficiary the value of the donated asset, this can be accomplished with the use of life insurance in a wealth replacement trust. This methodology will be thoroughly reviewed in Chapter 10.

COMBINED SALES AND GIFTS

As is readily evidenced in the example, the simple conversion of an appreciated asset into a charitable remainder trust to produce increased income makes good economic sense. This type of transaction can also be quite useful in a situation where investors are interested in acquiring another asset with the proceeds of a sale of part of the existing asset base. This type of transaction can be categorized as part sale, part charitable transfer.

Say, for example, that a couple has a security that has grown substantially in value. They wish to sell the security and take part of the proceeds from the transaction to purchase another security, which, in addition to providing a much larger income stream, could have some growth potential. They want to use the other portion of the proceeds from the sale to finance a lengthy trip they have been anticipating for a number of years.

The asset they are going to sell is valued at $1,000,000 and their cost basis in this security is $100,000. The new investment will require an expenditure of $750,000, which is less than what the sale of the current security will yield after federal capital gains tax. Luckily, they live in a state that does not have a state capital gains tax. This will not leave any funds, however, for their long anticipated trip to the Far East. The trip will probably run close to $100,000. In order to accomplish both objectives, an increased income and the long delayed trip, they decide to pledge the new security as collateral and borrow the necessary funds to finance their trip. This will cut into the future income from the new investment, as the loan interest and principal must be repaid. The other alternative is to put less into the new investment than they had originally planned.

A different alternative would involve the use of a charitable trust. A major tax advantage of the charitable remainder trust in addition to the elimination of the capital gains tax is the creation of a current income tax deduction. In this couple's situation, this would mean combining a gift into a charitable remainder trust of the entire $750,000 needed for the purchase of the new investment with an outright sale of enough of the securities to develop the funds needed to finance the extended vacation. The attendant income tax deduction that will result from the charitable remainder gift will be used to offset any capital gains taxes resulting from the outright sale of the securities.

Normally, a trust designed to fit this situation should have a deduction for the charitable gift substantial enough to fully offset any potential capital gains tax. This will result in the outright sale being significantly less than would have been required if the charitable remainder trust had not been utilized. Normally, the entire $250,000 of the remaining asset would not have to be liquidated; in fact, because of the income tax deduction generated by the gift, the actual liquidation will most likely be very close to the $100,000 needed. This would leave this couple with an additional $150,000 they can use for something else at a later date.

A very common problem for many company executives is the lack of diversification of their investments. This is an area of concern for many executives in larger U.S. corporations. To a great extent, the larger corporations have relied upon the use of stock options or bonuses to provide incentive compensation to their executives. In many cases, individual executives have ended up with an investment portfolio that is highly concentrated in one security. Quite often, not only their private investments are concentrated in this one stock but, also their assets in the company's profit sharing plan or their 401K program.

Investment diversity becomes a key concern for these executives. The financial pages of most major newspapers quite often feature major articles on a sale of a large block of stock acquired by an executive under a stock option program. The article usually details not only the total dollars involved in the transaction, but also the attendant capital gains tax paid. In many instances in recent years, a number of the taxable sales have been quite substantial. There have been very few reported situations where a charitable remainder trust was used for all or part of the exercise of the stock option. A small number of very large ones being established by donors were reported.

The average executive in a public company that has a stock option program as part of his or her compensation package may encounter a diversification problem. If this situation develops, the charitable remainder trust can be helpful. Transfer of the stock to a charitable remainder trust prior to sale will eliminate the capital gains tax on the appreciated value. The strategy of part sale, part charitable remainder trust transfer can also be utilized to put substantial dollars into the pocket of the executive with a much more favorable tax treatment than in an outright sale.

ESTATE TAX ELIMINATION

Another very creative strategy that can be utilized with a charitable remainder trust is in the area of estate taxes. It is possible with the utilization of a charitable remainder trust in conjunction with other traditional estate tax planning techniques to totally eliminate estate taxes upon the death of each spouse. In conventional estate planning, the estate taxes are calculated and current assets are either dedicated or new assets are created through the use of life insurance to fund the estate tax liability. In this approach, with estates consisting of substantial assets, combining the traditional planning technique of credit shelter trusts which pass each of the spouse's lifetime $600,000 exemptions with marital deduction trusts can have an impact. This effect is to delay or reduce the estate taxes due. The trust vehicle quite often used to provide all or the majority of the moneys needed to pay the actual taxes is the irrevocable life insurance trust. Life insurance that is not part of the decedent's estate is owned by the trust and is used to fund the estate taxes. This provides a methodology to pay the estate taxes, not eliminate them.

The combination of the above estate planning techniques with a charitable remainder trust can provide for total elimination of the estate taxes. In the majority of situations where this combination of trusts is utilized, the actual reduction of taxes will not be 100 percent, but it will be significant. This reduction restriction is due primarily to the planning restraints imposed on the advisors by individual family circumstances. The unique features of the charitable remainder trust add substantial flexibility to effective and efficient estate planning. Because of the significant changes and modifications that have occurred in the gift and estate tax field with the introduction of recent legislation, planning opportunities have been severely curtailed.

Utilizing the numerical facts in the first example in this chapter with a slight modification in the plan objectives will provide an opportunity to more closely examine this estate-planning technique. Instead of a conversion of the asset to provide for dollars to increase income, this situation will utilize a charitable remainder trust with more traditional estate planning to provide for total elimination of estate taxes and for passage of the entire estate to the next generation. The same $500,000 will be given to the charitable trust. The income that was being generated to the donor will remain the same. The additional income that is generated within the trust will be utilized to purchase a life insurance policy on the lives of both spouses that will be payable to the wealth replacement trust (irrevocable life insurance trust) at the death of the surviving spouse. Figure 5–1 illustrates the flow of monies.

As the figure illustrates, a series of steps must be taken in order for this arrangement to be fully implemented. The majority of these steps must be initiated by the couple's attorney with a variety of legal instruments. The majority of these actions can be summarized as follows:

1. A new will is drafted to cover the new planning process and any assets not flowing through the various trusts.

2. Marital deduction/credit shelter trusts are drafted for each spouse, establishing the $600,000 credit shelter trusts (Trust B)[1] for their children and the unlimited marital deduction trust for the surviving spouse (Trust A) at the first death.[2] These trusts also establish the estate gift of the entire estate of the survivor less the amount in the survivor's credit shelter trust to the charitable entity.

3. A wealth replacement trust (Trust D) is established to purchase the life insurance that will replace the estate assets at death.[3]

FIGURE 5–1
Charitable Estate Plan

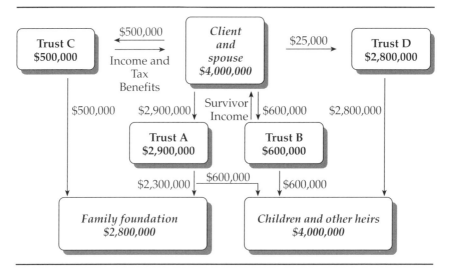

4. A charitable remainder trust (Trust C) is established to receive the initial gift of donated assets.[4]

5. A family foundation can also be established to act as the remainderman for the charitable remainder trust and also to receive the balance of the estate assets at the death of the surviving spouse.[5] This step is not necessary if a recognized charity is to act as the remainderman.

6. The wealth replacement trust (Trust C) applies for life insurance on the lives of the two spouses. Upon assurance that it will be issued, the necessary premium dollars are gifted into the trust.

7. The couple gift the $500,000 asset into the charitable remainder trust (Trust C).

8. The first-year tax savings created by the deduction for the gift to the charitable remainder trust (Trust C) is utilized to fund the gift into the wealth replacement trust (Trust D).

9. The notification letters are sent to each beneficiary of the wealth replacement trust (Trust D), describing their annual withdrawal period.[6] After the 30-day withdrawal period, the trustees

of the wealth replacement trust place the life insurance in force with the payment of the premium.

Depending on the individual circumstances, the attorney may add or delete from the above. These might seem like long, laborious tasks, but they can actually be instituted relatively quickly. Once the instruments are drafted and executed, the annual reporting procedures are very easy, provided the trustees have engaged a qualified administrative service. The majority of survivorship life insurance is illustrated and sold on a limited premium payment basis. Once this period of time has expired and the life insurance policy is performing as anticipated, the income beneficiaries can use the total dollar income generated by the investments in the charitable remainder trust in any manner they desire.

As can be seen, this estate planning technique can provide a very powerful tool in a comprehensive tax reduction strategy. The key to its proper adoption and utilization is the absolute necessity of comprehensive coordinated planning. This type of planning process cannot occur in a vacuum. It is extremely important that all parties involved in a process of this nature cooperate and coordinate.

The wealth replacement trust can be utilized to provide virtually any total amount of dollars to the selected beneficiaries. This amount could bear some relationship to the value of the asset donated to the charitable trust, or it could be any number selected by the donors. In the majority of the wealth replacement trusts done in conjunction with charitable remainder trusts, the amount selected for replacement to the heirs in the wealth replacement trust is the appreciated value of the assets the heirs would have received if the donors had held onto the property until their death. This value is normally the net value after the payment of estate taxes.

Hopefully, it is becoming apparent that the number of interesting financial, income, and estate tax planning techniques is constantly evolving as the planning community's understanding of the uses and coordination capabilities of the charitable remainder trust continually grows. One interesting aspect of charitable remainder trusts is that they can be instituted while the donor is alive (inter vivos) and at the donor's death (testamentary). This flexibility in design can lead to the development of interesting strategies. As with many things in life, quite often timing is an important consideration in charitable trust planning.

INVENTORY TRUSTS

It is often difficult to predict exactly when an asset will be sold. This inability often precludes the establishment of a charitable trust, as the trust document cannot be prepared in time. The regulations on sales being prearranged or committed prior to the establishment of the charitable trust further preclude any such daisy chain transactions. (These are arrangements that can be viewed as linked together.) To develop a solution to this timing issue, Renaissance, Inc., developed the concept of the *inventory trust*. In this arrangement, the charitable remainder trust is initially established with a modest gift. The legal, administrative, and reporting requirements are the same as any other charitable remainder trust. The administration fee as commensurate with the deposit is modest. The driving force behind this endeavor is the ability to establish the trust so that gifts may be made to it at a moment's notice.

The flexibility that the prior establishment of the charitable remainder trust allows the individual donor is enormous. Allowing timing to upset any future negotiations on the sale of assets intended to be gifted into a charitable remainder trust is no longer relevant once the adoption of an inventory trust has been completed. Quite often the sale of the asset is not negated, but, due to the unavailability of the inter vivos charitable remainder trust, the charitable gift never takes place. The sale is completed, yet the seller does not realize all that he or she could, and the charitable beneficiary receives nothing. Instead of this failure to maximize the return, minimize the tax consequences, and express a charitable intent, the seller ends up with less than maximum results.

The sale of an asset is often forced to take place at a specific time by circumstances well beyond the control of the individual owning the asset. An individual owns a large block of stock in a private company that is being sold at a specified date, and the timing of this transaction is of the essence. A real estate owner is approached by a large developer who wants to acquire a large track of land immediately, and if the sale is not agreed to within the next few days it will be lost. These and many other examples of financial transactions that require very quick responses illustrate the need for an "inventory trust" as part of an overall financial and estate plan. Having the trust in place to readily accept an asset before a sale is agreed upon or consummated can lend an incredible degree of flexibility to the financial situation. If the donor is also the party engaged in the selling negotiations, the added flexibility of having the charitable remainder trust already created and available can be significant. Different terms or arrangements of sale may be entered into to the owner's advantage when the seller of the stock can be a tax-exempt entity.

Another use of the inventory charitable remainder trust is for receipt of more modest contributions. Most organizations that administer charitable remainder trusts have minimum size requirements before they will accept the trust for administration. Charitable organizations that sponsor these types of programs and provide administration of the trusts as part of the gifting arrangement all require minimum trust size. Trust companies that provide administration as part of their trust services also have stated minimum trust size. As the administration of charitable remainder trusts can be quite expensive and time-consuming, all of these providers have set fairly high minimum size requirements. Most charitable organizations that do provide administration services have minimum size requirements that start at at least $100,000. Quite often, they are significantly higher. Trust company minimum size requirements normally start at $250,000. Some companies have minimum size requirements well into seven figures.

These minimum size requirements fail to provide trust availability to a large potential donor base that for a variety of reasons cannot meet this deposit criterion. The majority of the time, these potential donors end up not doing any form of charitable giving, and a potential long-term donor relationship is permanently lost. There are many valid reasons for a potential donor requiring the availability of an administrator who would service smaller contributions. These requirements would entail such arrangements as contributions being timed due to market or tax conditions. Another requirement might be the desirability of designing a program of annual gifts that would build to a larger sum.

CHARITABLE TRUSTS FOR ASSET ACCUMULATION

The curtailment of tax-advantaged accumulation programs, with the continual changes in federal income tax legislation, has prompted a search for methods of accumulating funds on a tax-favorable basis. The annual contribution program to a charitable remainder trust can offer an attractive alternative. It provides a methodology of accumulating assets in a tax-free environment with minimal dispersal of income. This can be accomplished with utilization of a net income with makeup charitable remainder unitrust (NIMCRUT). In this scenario, the trustee during the accumulation phase would invest in vehicles that produced no or little current income. When income is desired, the investments are switched into income-producing vehicles to provide the necessary distributions.

PROVIDING INCOME FOR OTHER FAMILY MEMBERS

Many potential candidates for charitable remainder trusts have financial obligations to other individuals, usually family members. Quite often, the individual receiving the funds will outlive the provider. This can create situations where the estate, another family member, or even the state in certain circumstances ends up with the financial support responsibility without the adequate funds required to guarantee an established style of living. The charitable remainder trust can offer an interesting alternative to the more conventional funding approaches.

There are a number of circumstances where the quality of life of the individual being provided with the income is somewhat or totally dependent on the ability of the individual provider to continue the stream of funds. Any disruption will have a direct effect on the lifestyle of the recipient. The individual affected could be a disabled or disadvantaged child, the parent of the provider, or a sibling or other relative. Providing for a related party can involve virtually all ages. The disabled or disadvantaged child could be relatively young or much older. Today's modern medicine can deal with many medical issues that in years past would have terminated life early. This longevity can promote extensive support issues both during the life and after the death of the income provider. In this set of circumstances, the charitable remainder trust can be a very interesting income tool.

Other related parties may be siblings or cousins, especially elderly ones who are living together as single, older adults. It has become more common, for example, for two older sisters to live together either after being widowed or having never married. Quite often, one of the parties has a significantly larger asset base than the other. A joint income beneficiary charitable remainder trust might be feasible to guarantee income to the survivor. A similar approach might be where the wealthier sister utilizes a testamentary charitable remainder trust to provide the necessary income stream to the surviving sister.

PROVIDING INCOME FOR NONFAMILY PARTIES

There are also instances when the individual needing the support is a nonrelated party, such as a long-term companion. There are situations where the continuation of an income stream or bequeathing assets to the survivor is desired. All too often, if this is not done in a protected legal fashion, the desired results may be subsequently undone by challenges to the arrangement in court by the decedent's heirs. The charitable remainder trust can prove a very useful tool in walling off the assets from legal challenge. In all these situations, supplying a steady source of funds that in the event of the death of the provider will not be interrupted and that will be relatively difficult to challenge from a legal standpoint will often be a paramount consideration.

There are certainly a number of well-documented situations where a provider's wishes are challenged and negated after death by other family members. Creating a charitable remainder trust for the individual who is in need of income, either as the primary or subsequent income beneficiary, is an extremely efficient method of addressing these issues. Not only has the required income been effectively provided, but a current income tax deduction has been created for the donor, and a charitable donation will ultimately be made to the donor's designated charity at the death of the income recipient. This provision of income can also relieve other family members of the obligation of providing future funds for the support of this individual.

Fashioning this type of charitable remainder trust while alive or at death does create special tax considerations. If the beneficiary of the income in a living trust situation is someone other than the donor or the donor's spouse, a gift of the annual trust income payments is created. This may not result in a gift tax being assessed, as the amount of the payment could possibly fall under the annual gift tax exemption. If it does not qualify, then either the gift tax due can be paid, or a portion of the lifetime exclusion can be used.

In the event that the charitable remainder trust is testamentary in nature, the income stream payable to the trust beneficiary will become for purposes of the estate tax calculation part of the estate of the decedent. This occurs due to the rules governing income in respect to a decedent. Assuming that the estate is large enough that at death it exceeds the lifetime $600,000 exclusion, estate taxes will be due. These taxes will be somewhat mitigated by the charitable estate tax deduction available to the estate for the value of the remainder interest being left to the charitable organization at the death of the income recipient.

In either the living or testamentary charitable remainder trust situation, the provision for income for another individual can provide relief from the uncertainty of the continuance of the income stream on the part of the recipient. This assurance of income can provide not only monetary assurance, but significant emotional assurance as well. The same emotional impact can be felt by the income provider. Many of these situations can be highly charged emotional ones, and guaranteeing the outcome of an obligation of this nature either on a living or testamentary basis can provide deep emotional satisfaction to the income provider. All of this can be done while at the same time ultimately providing a gift to the provider's designated charitable recipient.

A similar set of circumstances can evolve regarding an individual's long-term personal situation. One of the major, understated fears of older Americans is living too long and developing debilitating diseases that will require being institutionalized in a long-term care facility. The fear is not so much the institutionalization, but the quality of life once this has occurred. An additional concern is the fear of running out of money. Many older people feel that if the money runs out, the quality of the care will suffer. In many instances, the assets that an individual has can be quickly exhausted by long-term care expenses. Quite often, there is a requirement that upon admission to the institution the assets owned by the individual must be assigned to the institution to guarantee payment for services.

An alternative is a charitable remainder trust with assets that the individual can control prior to long-term medical problems developing. This trust will provide a stream of income either guaranteed or principal-based that will continue regardless of the state of the individual's health and that will produce income regardless of the status of the rest of the individual's assets. The corpus of the charitable remainder trust is not assignable. It cannot be attached by the institution. Provided the assets are properly invested, this stream of income from the charitable remainder trust will help to guarantee a quality of life to the individual that will provide much peace of mind. Many older individuals are also vitally interested in the concept of "giving something back." The ultimate dispersal of the remainder interest in a charitable trust can help satisfy that desire. If the organization that oversees or operates the long-term care facility is a recognized charity, it could even be the remainder beneficiary.

UTILIZING CHARITABLE TRUSTS TO PROVIDE ALIMONY AND CHILD SUPPORT PAYMENTS

Another issue can also be effectively addressed by the use of a charitable remainder trust. One lifestyle change that affects significant numbers of Americans is the dissolution of their marriage. Quite often, the separation agreement or divorce decree will stipulate an alimony payment to one of the parties. Under current income tax regulations, periodic alimony payments are deductible from income. In a number of cases, because of the earning power of one of the marriage partners, the amount of the alimony payments can be substantial.

Often, the alimony amounts can have a detrimental impact on the lifestyle of the marriage partner making the payments. The party responsible for the income payments will most likely have assets in addition to his or her earned income. Some of these assets may be suitable for gifting into a charitable remainder trust. This individual should also have an interest in charities or charitable causes. If there are low-yielding, highly appreciated assets in the portfolio, some of these can be contributed to a charitable remainder trust. The trust can then sell the assets and reinvest the proceeds in higher-income producing assets. The higher income stream can then be passed out to the donor/ income beneficiary in the form of trust income payments. The payments to the income beneficiary are received on a taxable basis. The alimony payments to the former spouse are tax deductible.

What has been created is a method of paying all or most of each required alimony installment from income that at the time of the divorce was nonexistent. These payments will therefore not have any impact on current lifestyle. The income tax liability on the payments from the charitable remainder trust will be offset by the amount of the deduction for the alimony payments. This can offer an attractive and creative solution to a normally unattractive problem.

This same type of solution can apply to child support payments. The difference in this arrangement is that child support payments are not tax deductible, so there would not be any deduction to offset the taxable income from the charitable remainder trust. The new income stream would be taxable, but unlike alimony there would be no direct offset as a deductible item. This income would still be from a source that did not exist prior to the creation of the charitable gift.

ASSET PROTECTION WITH CHARITABLE TRUSTS

Often, certain types of professionals or business owners are concerned about the exposure their personal assets experience due to certain business actions. In our litigious society, an individual's personal assets are subject to claim in the event of professional malpractice or business litigation. The major protection from loss in this type of litigation is a very large insurance policy or a very large capital base in the business. Quite often, the protection that a corporate form of business offers is not sufficient to protect the personal assets of the corporate owner. The piercing of the "corporate veil" by plaintiff's counsel has occurred on a few occasions in the recent past.

Walling off personal assets from this type of litigation is very difficult. One possible way to protect personal assets involves donated assets situated in charitable remainder trusts. As the creation and funding of charitable remainder trusts is irrevocable, the transfer of assets to it is difficult to undo. Donating assets into a charitable remainder trust to protect them from pending litigation or judgment could prove difficult to defend in court. However, assets donated to a charitable trust prior to any claim or litigation issues arising will be difficult for the litigant to recover. The vast majority of the time, the reason for establishing a charitable remainder trust is very far removed from the issue of protection of assets from litigation. In certain long-term planning situations, the fact that the assets of a charitable remainder trust can be protected from creditors is an added bonus.

COLLEGE FUNDING WITH CHARITABLE TRUSTS

Another creative use of a charitable remainder trust is the possible financing of a college education. Because of the enormous expenses associated with funding undergraduate and graduate studies, parents are often forced into a position of liquidating capital assets to fund these costs. Quite often, due to the capital gains tax on the appreciated value of the liquidated stock, an amount much larger than the tuition requirement must be sold. Instead of the parent personally liquidating the stock position, the creation of a charitable remainder income trust and the subsequent sale of the stock by the trust may present a more attractive alternative. The income percentage from the trust could be designed to fund the amount of college expenses plus the attendant taxes associated with the income.

When a child is very young, financial advisors will often suggest to the parents or the grandparents that they start to fund the college obligation with zero coupon bonds or other types of interest-bearing certificates. If these are taxable vehicles, taxes must be paid either from the income earned or from another source. If the investment vehicles are tax-exempt, the credited interest rate will be significantly less than the taxable equivalent. In either case, to reach the desired outcome will require either a longer accumulation period or a larger deposit than originally anticipated.

An alternative to this approach could be the establishment of a net income with makeup charitable remainder unitrust (NIM-CRUT). This could be funded with low or no dividend yielding stocks with significant growth potential, which can then be converted to income-producing vehicles in the years when the tuition funding is needed. The initial contributions into this trust can be staged over the first few years if the donors do not have readily available assets to contribute to the trust in the initial year. Once the college funding need has abated, the investment vehicles can be turned back to the accumulation mode unless a continuation of the income is warranted. The income flow can be started or stopped as desired and, of course, utilized for any purpose.

As has been illustrated in this chapter, the limitations on the varied uses of a charitable remainder trust to address the individual circumstances of a donor or potential donor are not as limiting as one would think. The development of creative problem-solving solutions in the proper application of charitable remainder trusts is also growing on a fast track. In all applications of these trust instruments, the charitable motivation is a key factor. Without the charitable factor, the resistance to the plan will be more entrenched, and the amount of the gift will be restrained.

Chapter Six
Business Applications

FAMILY OWNED BUSINESS TRANSFERS

The largest single category of assets controlled by many people over 50 in the United States, is family owned businesses.[1] The wealth that has been built in family owned and controlled businesses is enormous. Some of these businesses may now be public companies, but their origins rest with individual families. These businesses are represented in every industry and profession, from farmers, machine operators, and financiers to the most skilled physicians. There are many differences between the types of businesses, the ownership, the business entity, and the dreams and aspirations of the founders, but they also share many traits.

The most common trait they share is the lack of liquidity for the value of the business. A sole proprietorship, partnership, or close corporation is not as readily salable as a publicly traded company. When the owner wishes to expand the business, the options of obtaining the capital needed are not as broad as those offered to a public company. A more restrictive scenario, most likely, will be encountered when the owner wishes to retire, becomes disabled, or dies, the last two being the most restrictive of all. An intrinsic part of the value of any closely held business is the worth of the owner to that business. Many times, almost the entire value of the business is the worth of the owner. This is certainly true in virtually every sole proprietorship or one-person corporation. Quite often, the business is so intertwined with the individual that once something happens to the individual the value of the business dramatically suffers. Many times, the valuation is irreparably destroyed.

In the event that the business owner wishes to sell the business while alive, the ability to receive a full market value for her or his interest is readily attainable. Usually there are provisions in the sales contracts that call for the current owner to perform certain tasks to assure the smooth transition of the business to the new owners. Such is not normally the case in the event of the disability or death of the current owner. If the business doesn't die with the incapacity or death of the owner, it surely suffers. In either case, it is much more difficult for the family to realize a true market value in these circumstances. In all these situations, the disability of the owner can present a very difficult financial situation to the family, but the death of the owner usually presents the most financial challenges.

VALUATION

In many pieces of tax legislation, Congress has recognized the intrinsic value of the family owned business to the country. The primary issue that Congress has addressed revolves around the transfer of the business to another family member or some other party, while alive or at death. A number of Internal Revenue Code sections have been created and modified over the years to assist in the transfer of these businesses.[2] Every one of these sections has dealt with the issues of valuation and how to pay the taxes at the time of transfer, the two major problems encountered in the transfer of closely held businesses. The valuation questions are a major issue, as are the payment of either the conversion or transfer tax at the time of sale or bequest.

Most litigation that occurs with the Internal Revenue Service in this area revolves around the question of the value of the business or closely held stock at the time of transfer or death. The number of cases in these areas is enormous, and with all the changes in the rules and regulations in the last few tax acts, the backlog of cases is mounting. Valuation questions can pose enormous problems for a decedent's estate when the Internal Revenue Service raises the issue. Quite often, the estate's appraisal and the IRS's appraisal are quite different, with the estate normally being the lower of the two. This continual problem is what causes virtually all of the litigation questions. In all of this, the issue of how to pay the often enormous transfer taxes is left unanswered. If proper planning had been instituted prior to the event triggering the need, the question would not be unanswered.

In a number of situations, the major roadblock to doing effective income and estate tax planning with family or closely held business owners is the significant taxes that are generated by a sale or transfer. Quite often, a major question arises that has nothing to with taxes or transfer costs. This is a psychological and emotional issue involving control. The individual or family that has seen a business grow and prosper often identifies quite closely with the business; in fact, in some situations the business becomes their lives. They practice the "nobody can do it better than me" school of thought. Separating them from the business can often be quite traumatic. Turning it over to a child or children can be paramount to a disaster. Effectively dealing with this issue is quite often more challenging than minimizing the tax consequences of the transaction. In both these areas, the charitable remainder trust can be an effective planning aid.

If an individual business owner were to donate her or his interest in a business directly to a charitable organization the organization would either immediately sell the business or refuse the gift. Organizations do not, except in very rare circumstances, have the ability to operate a business. In addition to the problems of actually directing the gift to a charitable organization, the gift may do little to address the overall income and estate planning issues. The gift may solve the problem of the estate taxes due on the asset, but, the gift does nothing to address the other issues. In fact, the overall result may be detrimental to the family's long-term financial viability. In many family owned businesses, the income derived by the family, and in many situations the extended family, is a vital part of the family's current and future wealth. Without proper planning, there can be a very detrimental impact upon this wealth when a transfer of ownership is desired or forced to happen.

CHARITABLE REMAINDER TRUST ALTERNATIVE

An attractive alternative to many of the traditional planned and unplanned transfers of family and closely held businesses is the use of a charitable remainder trust as the intermediary in the transaction. Proper use of a charitable remainder trust in business transfer and succession planning can add immeasurable value to the actual transaction. The other important issue that can often be addressed is the provision for the current owner to retain control. Depending on the individual circumstances, the current business owner may retain effective control of the business while serving in the role of the trustee of the charitable remainder trust. In actual plan design, this can be important in attaining the approval of the key figures. The emphasis on the ability of the current owner to act as the trustee of the charitable remainder trust is not to be underemphasized. It is often the critical piece to a successful completion of the planning process.

Exactly how the charitable remainder trust enters into the transfer or succession planning process can vary from situation to situation. As the advisor becomes more experienced in the use of charitable remainder trusts, the areas of involvement will be more varied. This is one area where virtually every situation is different, although in the majority of instances the desired outcomes are the same. One detriment to a number of business sales occurring is after entering into a discussion of the possible sale of the business, the owner then starts to consider the impact of the capital gains tax due on the appreciated value. If the business has been successful, the appreciation will often be quite significant. When the size of the actual tax is calculated, the owner objects to paying it, and the pending sale is negated. There are some installment payments and stock swaps that can be used to delay or lessen the tax burden, but they should only be utilized in the right set of circumstances. Often, their use does not result in less tax being paid, but only in a timed or delayed payment of the amounts due. These tactics do not result in the ultimate avoidance of the taxes. In this endeavor, the charitable remainder trust can prove extremely beneficial.

The charitable remainder trust can be the recipient of the stock in a family controlled business as long as the corporation is a regular corporation. S corporation stock cannot be placed in a charitable remainder trust. A trust cannot be a shareholder in an S corporation.[3] Once the stock is donated to the charitable remainder trust, the trustees are responsible for voting that stock at the annual meeting. In a large number of family run businesses, the continuation of the firm by one or more members of the family at the retirement or death of the current owner is often desired. How to accomplish this in a tax-advantaged manner is often of paramount concern.

In the case of retirement or sale, the transfer will trigger tax consequences for the seller. Where the corporation has built up a large amount of retained earnings for the purpose of redeeming corporate stock and when the redemption takes place, a capital gains tax will be due. If the stock is first transferred to a charitable remainder trust and then redeemed from the trust, the capital gains tax will be eliminated. This provides an excellent methodology of transferring capital from the corporate pocket to the individual without any drain from taxes.

Prior to the transfer, the value of each share is diluted by the number of outstanding shares. If shares are transferred to another family member prior to the gifting of the stock to the charitable remainder trust, they will be either gifted or sold at the diluted price. Once the shares are gifted to the charitable remainder trust and then subsequently redeemed by the corporation, they become treasury stock, and the value of the outstanding shares will increase proportionately, equal to the value of the shares that were redeemed. This creates added value to the use of the charitable remainder trust in these circumstances.

The owner of the shares that are gifted to a charitable remainder trust avoids the capital gains tax on the redemption transaction, and the other family member, usually of a subsequent generation, has previously acquired shares at a value that will be greatly enhanced by the redemption of the donated shares. This plan works well with companies that have the ability to develop retained earnings. It will work in the same fashion even if the funds for the redemption are not readily available. In the right situation, financing of the redemption may be obtained by the corporation from outside sources. The outcome from the tax standpoint would be the same for the individuals; however, the corporation would be in a different financial picture. The corporation would now have debt to reimburse, which might affect the value of the remaining outstanding shares. For those that cannot, for various reasons, create the necessary pool of funds and have to borrow from a bank to finance the redemption, there are other alternatives.

One of the alternatives is to effect the transfer along the lines of a traditional buy-and-sell agreement. In this arrangement, the current owners sell, and the new owners purchase the business or the corporate stock. This can be done in a lump sum purchase or with periodic payments. For tax purposes, the current owners recognize as gain the amount of the sale price that exceeds their investment in the business. As this transaction is a capital one, the new owners purchase the business or the corporate stock with after-tax funds. This type of transaction happens thousands of times each day across the country. The tax drain on the current owners can prove detrimental to more sales occurring. Because of the large percentage of the sale price going to taxes, it can also have an adverse impact on the future lifestyle of the sellers, especially if the sellers are retiring and are going to be dependent on these funds for a large part of their retirement income.

Provided the sellers are attuned to the concept, a much more tax-efficient method of addressing this type of transaction is to interject a charitable remainder trust into the situation prior to any sale or agreement for sale being made. Not only does the tax situation dramatically improve, but the yield to the sellers from the sale increases expeditiously. In addition to the actual increase in dollars to the sellers, an endowment fund will be made available for their favorite charity. In many buy-sell situations, the current owners are disposing of the business or corporate stock because of either a change in the business climate or a change in their personal situation. Quite often, the change is of a personal nature. These personal changes often result in the sellers needing to realize a good return on the proceeds of the sale in order to provide the income needed to support a future lifestyle. Using the charitable remainder trust as an intermediary in the sale transaction will provide for a dramatic increase in inevitable sale proceeds.

Using the charitable remainder trust as the recipient of the gift of the business or the stock is a viable procedure in a sales situation with an outside party or a family member. The identity of the purchaser is immaterial in this type of situation. Due to the aging of the parent, in many cases the buyer is a child of the current owner. The effect of the charitable remainder trust being the seller of the stock rather than the parent is immaterial to the child. The child's purchase price and tax considerations will be the same. The difference will be the increased proceeds of the sale realized on behalf of the parent. This could develop into an added long-term benefit for the child, as the increased proceeds the parent realizes on the sale will produce additional income. This could well serve to lessen any future financial need on the part of the parent and, in turn, financial obligation on the part of the child.

PARTIAL TRANSFERS TO CHARITABLE REMAINDER TRUSTS

In business sale situations, the sellers often want to obtain a block of capital to invest or spend on something of importance. In this case, the transfer of the business, in total, to the charitable remainder trust would be in deference to that desire. An alternative is to sell part of the business and transfer the other part into the charitable remainder trust. The portion that is sold will generate a capital gains tax based upon the appreciated value. The portion that is donated into the charitable trust will generate a tax deduction based upon the calculation factors used to compute the value of the remainder interest. The challenge quite often in these situations is to have the capital gains tax and the charitable deduction as equal as possible. In the majority of situations, even if the numbers cannot be equalized, the availability of the charitable deduction to offset a portion of the capital gains tax is of immeasurable help in closing the sale.

INVESTMENT TRANSFERS TO CHARITABLE REMAINDER TRUSTS

The flexibility that the use of the charitable remainder trust can lend in these circumstances can be very useful. An installment sale of the business or the stock can be matched with a like installment transfer to the charitable trust. The value of the charitable income tax deduction in helping to structure a sales pattern favorable to the seller is restricted only by the inventiveness of the parties involved. A major component of the calculation of the charitable remainder trust deduction is the distribution rate that will be used to disperse income to the beneficiaries. The higher the payout rate, the lower the deduction; the lower the payout rate, the higher the deduction. If the circumstances of the particular sale and gift situation warrant a certain deduction, a number of calculations can be made to determine the best distribution rate to obtain the desired deduction. This can often be matched with the correct style of charitable remainder trust to create an extremely attractive solution to the seller of the stock or business.

This type of approach does not have to be limited to a business sale situation. It can be utilized in a number of sale and gift programs involving virtually any type of asset. It normally is most effective with a seller who has the ability to understand all the ramifications of the combined transaction. It also requires a seller who is charitably motivated and realizes the value of his or her actions. As in all charitable remainder trust situations, the plan will only work if you have a donor/seller who is or becomes charitably motivated. Without this motivation, even though the plan makes incredible economic sense, the plan will not be executed. If it is and the charitable motivation was really nonexistent, the administration and actualization of the plan will prove extremely difficult. If the charitable motivation is not evident during the planning phase, it is much better to abandon the charitable concept and implement an alternative plan than to proceed.

EMPLOYEE STOCK OWNERSHIP TRANSFERS

As was previously mentioned, sales of a business or stock interest can be effected with nonrelated parties just as easily (in fact, in many cases more easily) as with relatives. One potential source of business purchasers are the employees of the company. More and more, the employees of companies are becoming actively involved, not only in the management of the business, but also in its ownership. This can be accomplished by an outright purchase of the business by an employee or a group of employees or through the use of an employee stock ownership plan (ESOP). Whether the employees purchase the business outright or through the ESOP, a charitable remainder trust can be interjected into the transaction to act as the seller of the stock. This will provide added tax advantages to the current stock owner with no impact upon the purchasers.

A direct purchase of the business by the employees from a donated interest in a charitable remainder trust operates the same as a purchase by a family member or another outside party. The employees need the funds necessary to make the purchase. These can come from the employees themselves or from an outside source. In either case, the effect would be the same upon the charitable remainder trust. The business interest would be purchased from the charitable remainder trust and the proceeds reinvested to provide income for the donor. Depending upon the percentage of the business interest purchased, the employees would either control the business or be minority owners.

In the circumstances where an employee stock ownership plan would be a party to the transaction, the exact relationship between the owner and the employees is not as clear-cut. An ESOP can be a valuable tool in a variety of financial planning situations. Among its many applications are such items as the sale of a business interest, raising capital for the company, providing a methodology for the retirement of the current business owner, and funding company retirement programs. The ESOP legislation was established in 1974 under the Employee Retirement Income Security Act to provide a tax incentive for the spread of company stock ownership among the employees of the company.[4] The basic thrust of the legislation was to give employees a financial stake in the companies in which they were employed. The companies would then become more participative and in turn more productive and profitable. Congress has enhanced this legislation a number of times since 1974. Recent years have seen the enactment of a number of these incentive plans.

ESOPs in actual practice bear a strong resemblance to profit-sharing plans; in fact, a number of profit-sharing plans have been converted to ESOPs. The major differences are that ESOPs by their very nature are comprised primarily of the employer's stock. The contributions by the corporation are either in corporate stock or in cash. The ESOP is even allowed to borrow funds to purchase stock. This privilege can invoke some very interesting planning discussions between the corporate owner and the Trustees of the ESOP. The trustees in virtually every case comprise the owner and an employee committee. One of the major advantages of the ESOP from the corporate owner's perspective is its ability to provide a means of liquefying the normally illiquid corporate owned stock. The ESOP is a very flexible financial instrument. A number of financial advisors have been very innovative in the application of ESOPs to individual situations. It would be impossible to explore all of these possibilities. The following example is a more detailed explanation of the combination of a charitable remainder trust and an ESOP.

An individual corporate owner wants to dispose of a portion of his close corporation stock but does not want to bring in any outside buyers. The owner also wishes to do this in the most tax-efficient manner. The financial advisor suggests that the current corporate profit-sharing plan be converted to a corporate ESOP plan. The profit-sharing plan has assets of almost $800,000. The corporation has a value of $5,000,000, and the sole owner wishes to liquefy 20 percent of this. As there are restrictions, based upon a percentage of total employee compensation, on the amount of stock that can be contributed to an ESOP in any given year, it might be impossible to convert all of the stock in one year. As the advisor reviews the plan calculations with the owner, this limitation does not appear to present a problem. The profit-sharing plan has $800,000 of assets, and the corporation could contribute the balance of the $1,000,000, or the ESOP could borrow the $200,000 shortfall from the local bank to effect the entire purchase.

The major stumbling block in this arrangement is voiced by the stockholder when the capital gains tax due on the transfer is raised. The owner had been under the mistaken impression that no taxes were due upon the transfer. The advisor happens to know the client well and is aware of the youngest child's severe medical problems and the owner's strong emotional attachment to the hospital that is treating the child. The advisor suggests that a charitable remainder trust be interjected into the situation as a possible solution.

The charitable remainder trust would be given the $1,000,000 in stock. The children's hospital would be the remainder beneficiary at the death of the owner and spouse. As the corporate stock pays no dividends, a way of liquefying the stock would be needed. The ESOP has or can acquire the necessary funds to effect the purchase from the charitable trust. If the ESOP borrows moneys to help finance the purchase, the repayment of this loan with future tax deductible corporate contributions will result in both the interest and the principal repayment being paid with tax deductible funds.

The trustees of the trust can use the proceeds of the sale to invest in income-producing vehicles that will provide a new stream of income for the owner and spouse. The owner will avoid any capital gains on the sale of the stock while at the same time creating a significant income tax deduction that can be used to offset annual income in the current year and for five years into the future. This is usable until it is fully expended. If needed, the owner can divert a portion of the income tax savings and new annual income payments into an irrevocable life insurance trust that can purchase life insurance on both spouses to provide added liquidity at death for estate tax purposes. This innovative combination of financial plans addresses all of the concerns raised by the owner and provides significant additional benefits that further enhance the viability of the solution.

There are a few more interesting planning considerations in this example. The owner, who is also an employee, is most likely the highest paid employee of the corporation. As contributions of both cash and stock are made to the ESOP, a portion, most likely a large portion, of each contribution is being allocated to the owner's account. Therefore, the stock that was gifted by the owner to the charitable trust and subsequently sold to the ESOP is being returned to the owner via the accrual of the vested benefit in ESOP. Ultimately, the individual participants in the ESOP will reach retirement age. At retirement, the plan has to provide, if requested, full redemption of the shares credited to the retiring participant. This can be done from funds in the ESOP or by having the shares purchased by another party. The corporation could redeem the shares from the retiree. The shares may also be purchased by a child of the owner, thus passing the stock to a future generation.

EMPLOYEE STOCK OWNERSHIP PLAN— SUMMARY

This methodology will allow the entire planning process to come full circle:

1. The parent and current stockholder donates the shares to a charitable remainder trust.
2. In return for the charitable donation, the owner receives a current income tax deduction.
3. The owner avoids any capital gains on the gift transaction.
4. The ESOP acquires the stock from the charitable remainder trust without any tax consequences.
5. The charitable remainder trust invests the funds to produce income for the income beneficiaries of the trust.
6. When the employees, including the owner, retire, the employee stock ownership plan either disperses the stock in the account to the employee or converts the stock into distributable cash. The owner, as an employee of the corporation and a participant in the ESOP, receives at retirement, as the distributable share of the plan, his or her portion of the stock that had been originally transferred to the charitable remainder trust.
7. The stock could be redeemed by the corporation, an outside party, or the heirs of the former owner of the shares.
8. When the children purchase the stock, a tax deductible capital gains free transfer of a portion of the business value to a subsequent generation has been effected.
9. All transactions in the above scenario are to be handled at arm's length in order to remove any question of party-at-interest violations.

In the event of the death of the owner and spouse, the life insurance proceeds of the irrevocable life insurance trust could also be utilized to purchase the stock from the nonfamily members who retire under the plan auspices. Thus the possibility of addressing a number of potential estate and succession planning issues can be accomplished with this innovative combination of plans. The variations that can be obtained with the proper utilization of different planning techniques can prove extremely useful to the financial advisor.

CONVERSION OF INCOME

Another interesting application of a charitable remainder trust in a stock ownership situation is the ability that is available in the correct circumstances to turn ordinary income into a charitable deduction.[5] In the case of publicly traded and close corporation securities, there is a period of time between the declaration date of a dividend and the date it is actually credited to the stock. If the stock is sold during this period of time, the seller does not recognize the dividend as income. The dividend belongs to the buyer, who in turn recognizes the dividend as income. The value of the stock when sold, however, is increased to include the unpaid dividend. Thus, in this situation, the seller has converted an ordinary income tax situation into a capital gains tax.

The rules that apply to the stock sale can also be applied to the gift of stock to a charitable remainder trust. By gifting a stock during the period of time between the declaration and the record date, the donor can receive a charitable tax deduction for the declared but unpaid dividend. On the recording date for the dividend payment, the owner of the stock will be the charitable trust and will be the dividend income recipient. The inflated value of the stock during this period of time can add significantly to the amount of the charitable gift and in turn the corresponding charitable deduction. In the right set of circumstances, this approach can prove very useful to the individual stockholder and the financial advisor.

CORPORATE TAKEOVERS AND LIQUIDATIONS

A somewhat similar situation can exist with corporate stock, primarily publicly traded stock, where transactions are occurring that will result in ordinary income or capital gains being recognized by the individual shareholder. Such incidents can occur in corporate takeovers or liquidations. In the majority of takeovers and liquidations, the individual shareholder has little or no control over the outcome. In many cases, the income tax consequences of corporate takeovers or liquidations are very adverse to the individual stockholder. One creative way of avoiding these adverse circumstances is to contribute the corporate owned stock to a charitable remainder trust prior to the takeover or liquidation. The timing of the contribution is important in order to guarantee that the gift transaction will be without tarnish.

In the case of the corporate takeover, it is essential that the stock be gifted to the charitable trust prior to the actual occurrence of any offer being accepted by the current shareholder. In many corporate takeover situations, there is an element of cash involved. The cash could be for a portion of the purchase price or for the entire amount. In public companies, takeovers are preceded by a tender offer that spells out the terms of the purchase. The gift of stock must be completed and in the hands of the trustee before any tender offer can be accepted.[6] If this does not occur in time, the actual sale of the stock and the attendant appreciation will be allocated to the individual stockholder, with the attendant income tax consequences, not to the charitable trust.

When a liquidation is going to take place, the income tax consequences to the individual shareholder may be severe. The avoidance of that income would certainly prove beneficial to the individual stockholder. If the stock is contributed to a charitable remainder trust by the individual shareholder, the income tax consequences can be avoided, since whatever tax consequences do occur will transpire in the tax-exempt environment. As in the takeover situation, the timing of the gift is critical. The key timing requirement is that the transfer to the charitable remainder trust must take place before the final liquidation vote is taken by the board of directors. Once the final vote is taken, the liquidation is a fait accompli, and the resultant income must be recognized by the individual stockholder.[7]

Consideration must also be given as to whether the individual stock involved in the liquidation is a proper gift for the charitable remainder trust. In all the financial transactions, the suitability of the vehicle being donated must be considered. Stock that may be going through a liquidation process and will end up with little or no value cannot be converted into an asset that can produce income for the charitable trust income beneficiary. There is absolutely no valid economic reason to donate this type of asset into a charitable remainder trust. Most importantly, there is no value to the charity. If there were going to be an economic value to the stock, however, there might be a charitable purpose for the donation.

SALES TO THE CORPORATION

There may be situations where close corporation stock is given to a charitable remainder trust and, for whatever reason, cannot be readily sold. The stock may also not pay any annual dividends. The only buyer that can be found for the stock is the donor, who is also the former stockholder or the close corporation itself. In the right set of circumstances, this could prove a valuable financial planning tactic. If the donor wants income from the trust, liquefying the trust stock is essential. The owner's acquisition basis will be the current purchase price. If the needed income is for spousal support, liquidation is essential. If the corporation has a surplus of cash, the liquidation of the stock by the corporation could be utilized to effect a tax-advantaged transfer of monies from the corporation to the benefit of the stockholder. In many cases, the donor/stockholder owns all or a majority of the outstanding shares, and the value of these shares would remain essentially unchanged by a corporate redemption of its own stock. As in all of these planning ideas, the proper use and circumstances for correct execution are essential.

CORPORATE ASSET TRANSFERS

A need may also develop for a corporation to sell or dispose of a certain asset or assets. Instead of a sale or liquidation of the asset, a gift to a charitable remainder trust may be appropriate.

The charitable remainder trust created by a corporation is a term-certain trust. It can run for a period of up to 20 years.[8] There are a number of uses for a charitable remainder trust in a corporate framework. The tax treatment of a corporate contribution to a charitable remainder trust can often fall under the scrutiny of the Internal Revenue Service. This is especially true in closely held corporations where there is only one stockholder. If the contributions of the corporation solely serve the purposes of the individual stockholder, that contribution will run the risk of being cast as a dividend. This requires careful scrutiny of all corporate gifts to charitable remainder trusts, in order to assure the shareholders of a solid tax footing.

A more liberal view is taken for corporate contributions on the behalf of employees. There are a number of corporations, both closely held and publicly owned, that offer their employees charitable gift-matching programs. An employee gift to a recognized charitable organization can result in an equal contribution being made by the corporation. A corporation can also make a direct contribution on behalf of the employee, at the employee's direction. The employee receives no income tax consequences from the gift. The same set of circumstances would hold true for a gift to a charitable remainder trust on behalf of an employee. The employee would receive no current income tax consequences on the gift but would be responsible for the income taxes due on receipt of the income from the charitable trust. Naturally, as in all of these types of arrangement, care must be exercised in keeping the entire transaction at arm's length.[9]

If the stock that is going to be gifted to the charitable remainder trust is stock in a closely held corporation, certain appraisal requirements will be mandated. The rules for appraisal of closely held stock are basically the same as those for other hard-to-value assets. There is a basic appraisal threshold of $5,000 for hard-to-value assets. At this level, a qualified appraisal must be attached to the income tax return claiming the deduction. For closely held stock, the qualified appraisal requirement starts at the $10,000 level. Between $5,000 and $10,000, the donor need only attach an appraisal summary to the income tax return. In spite of this exception, it is good practice to have qualified appraisals for all gifts of hard-to-value assets.[10]

Chapter Seven

Retirement Planning Applications

THE QUALIFIED RETIREMENT PLAN

Over the last few decades, one of the financial planning tools most utilized by the small and medium-sized business owner has been the qualified retirement plan. Once a business had adopted a basic health insurance program, the next benefit program to be enacted by a business was a retirement plan. The full deductibility of contributions to the plan from the business income taxes spurred growth across the country. The tax-deferred growth of the assets within the plan was also a significant reason for their popularity. As the proliferation of retirement plans continued, Congress and the Treasury Department began to enact a series of legislative changes that dramatically altered the rules under which the plans were adopted and operated.

Many of the rule changes were adopted to curb supposed abuses of the retirement system, both real and exaggerated. Starting in 1974 with the Employee Retirement Income Security Act (ERISA), legislation brought about a number of dramatic changes in the way in which the retirement plans were calculated, enacted, administered, reported, and distributed. A major problem that plan sponsors encountered was an almost constantly changing regulatory environment. Just when a previously enacted set of regulations were adopted, a new legislative initiative became law, and the rules of plan operation changed once again. Even the Internal Revenue Service had a great deal of difficulty keeping up with the changes. They were often three to five years behind in drafting the regulations and procedures required to interpret the new legislation.

The volumes of legislation bore such names as Tax Reform Act of 1976 (TRA'76), Economic Recovery Tax Act of 1981 (ERTA), Tax Equity and Fiscal Responsibility Act of 1982 (TEFRA), Tax Reform Act of 1984 (TRA'84), Tax Reform Act of 1986 (TRA'86), Omnibus Budget Reconciliation Act of 1986 (OBRA'86), and OBRA'89, '90, and '93. Sandwiched in between these pieces of legislation were numerous other tax code revisions. For the most part, each of these legislative actions caused a reduction or curtailment in the number and scope of the plans being sponsored by U.S. corporations. The impact was especially severe in the smaller corporate and professional plans. In these type of organizations, one of the largest personal assets the business owner possessed was the value of the vested pension plan. As plans were either terminated or curtailed, business owners searched for alternative ways to both accumulate and tax shelter their assets.

The unfortunate consequence of all these changes and increased plan administrative costs was a dramatic curtailment in the number of retirement plans being funded and enacted by business owners as well as a major switch in plan design from the traditionally defined benefit pension plan to the defined contribution plans. A defined benefit plan calculation is based upon a benefit being predetermined at retirement and moneys set aside each year based upon actuarial calculations that will accumulate at retirement to a required sum that will provide the necessary retirement benefit. A defined contribution plan is based upon a percentage of the employee's salary being set aside each year. This percentage contribution will accumulate to a sum at normal retirement that will provide an income to the retiree. Because the actual dollars that will be set aside each year cannot accurately be determined, as they are based upon future salaries, the final benefit at retirement cannot be precisely predicted.

As the rules and regulations became more stringent, every individual in the country earning more than $150,000 was affected. This level of income became the maximum amount available for retirement plan calculation purposes. This reduction in compensation levels led to further restriction on the retirement plans in many smaller organizations. In larger companies, it led to a significant increase in the number of organizations installing nonqualified deferred compensation plans for these employees. In the companies that already had such arrangements, the number of participants dramatically increased.

Another problem was the creation by the various legislative acts of fully funded and overfunded defined benefit plans. As the majority of business owners and professionals in their late 40s or early 50s had enacted defined benefit plans, the curtailment of contributions was enormous, and the termination of these plans accelerated. These individuals could no longer contribute to the pension plan without running afoul of the penalties attached to excess plan accumulations, penalties that are very severe and difficult to avoid.

One of the popular solutions initially presented was the 401(k) retirement plan.[1] This type of retirement plan was promoted and designed as a vehicle to encourage employee participation and savings. Many large corporations quickly adopted 401(k) plans either in addition to or in place of other retirement programs. This resulted in a cost shifting of some of the funding of retirement benefits onto the shoulders of the individual employees. In the past, the majority of plan funding obligations had been borne by the corporation. These type of plans proved very popular in larger corporations, especially those with a young average-employee age base. The younger employees could see both more short-term vesting occurring as well as a larger projected benefit at retirement. Further legislative enactments have begun to dampen the enthusiasm.

The picture is more cloudy in the smaller business and professional area. Here, because of the size of the employee groups and the larger divergence of salaries between different employee categories, the 401(k) was not as easily accepted. The increased cost of administration of this type of plan was also prohibitive for many organizations. These points not withstanding, a number of firms started 401(k) plans only to see them flounder in the first few years due to lack of participation and regulatory changes.

Business owners as well as professionals started to search for other tax-favored investments. Many sought out real estate and other types of tax shelters. These often became a problem for the investor, as the underlying economics in many situations was nonexistent. Congress also enacted major legislative reform that precluded the shelters from existing. Many small business owners and professionals were left with little or no sheltering capability for the accumulation of assets. Although Congress wanted to contain the abuses, they also dramatically affected many legitimate programs.

The business owner as well as the professional in many instances had totally lost the capability of sheltering any assets on a tax-deductible basis. Any investments that were made in tax-free municipal bonds and both fixed and variable annuities had to be made with after-tax contributions. In addition, annuities faced surrender penalties if any withdrawals occurred prior to age 59 1/2. Some of the professionals affiliated with hospitals and other charitable organizations could contribute on a tax-favorable basis to pooled income funds.[2] However, two major issues attendant to pooled income funds were the inability on the part of the donor to direct the nature of the investment and the immediate income tax recognition of the income as received. The pooled income program did not offer the donor the ability to accumulate moneys for use in later years.

CHARITABLE REMAINDER TRUST ALTERNATIVE

At the same time the changes were occurring in the pension regulations, the charitable remainder trust was emerging as a financial planning tool. As has been discussed, the traditional use of a charitable remainder trust has been the conversion of a highly appreciated asset into an income stream. One type of charitable remainder trust that does lend itself to being an accumulation mechanism is the net income with makeup unitrust (NIM-CRUT).[3] In this charitable remainder trust, tax-deductible donations are made; the trustee instructs the money manager on the type of investments in which the trust should invest. The deductions for the contributions are based upon the normal factors affecting a charitable remainder trust deduction: the age of the donor, the income payout factor, and the federal midterm interest rate at the time of the gift. The investment directions from the trustee will stipulate that the funds are to be directed into securities of organizations whose primary objective is growth.

Income is a secondary issue. In fact, during the accumulation phase, the less income the better. The total emphasis should be on growth of the trust assets.

Once the accumulation phase has been completed, the trustee can direct the money manager to switch the investment strategy from growth-oriented vehicles to income-type instruments. Income becomes the motivating factor in the investment strategy. As the income stream is generated within the charitable trust, the income beneficiary can make up the prior year's missed income distributions. These missed distributions are based upon the specified percentage payout being applied to the accumulation amount on each annual valuation date. Any income payments that had previously been distributed are naturally subtracted from the income shortage during the calculation phase. The detail and thoroughness of these calculations are one of the primary reasons a sophisticated trust administration firm is needed to track the required figures.

It took only a little inspired imagination to remove the NIM-CRUT from its classic application to one that could provide a viable alternative to those business owners and professionals who were seeking an alternative tax-favored accumulation structure to the curtailed or terminated pension program. A few key elements of the overall pension alternative strategy must be in place for the NIMCRUT to be an effective tool in the planning process. The trust must allow for the donor to act in the role of the trustee or cotrustee. This is the only way to assure that the investment strategy will be properly adopted and followed. The investment strategy is key to allowing the whole process to actually follow the plan design.

Another necessary element is an investment manager who understands the goals that have been established and who also has a basic understanding of the workings and investment guidelines for a charitable remainder trust. Another required element is a trust administrator who can adjust his or her supervision procedures to handle NIMCRUTs with small to modest deposits, including all of the varied annual reporting, calculation, and valuation requirements. The administrator also must have a fee structure that can support modest deposits and not prove cost prohibitive to the plan. If the administrator does not have a fee structure that is supportive to the design of the charitable trust, the entire integrity of the overall plan can be jeopardized. For anyone other than a professional plan administrator to attempt to provide administration services to a charitable trust of this nature would be foolhardy and most likely result in the entire plan coming under scrutiny. The asset-tracking tasks alone would prove a daunting task for anyone without a sophisticated administration system. Without these provisos, the charitable remainder trust will have a difficult time living up to the plan design and will prove highly unsatisfactory to the donor. However, with these issues addressed, the plan will prove to be a very beneficial one to all parties concerned.

The typical individual who would partake in this type of program is one who not only needs to accumulate assets for retirement but who has a desire to ultimately help an organization or institution in which she or he has a strong interest. As a tax-deduction vehicle the instant reaction from a number of prospects and clients is a negative one because of the low percentage of the contribution that is deductible. As many of the individuals who will be entering into these arrangements are younger than the traditional charitable remainder trust candidate, the percentage tax deduction is initially modest. Two considerations can address that concern. First, although the initial percentage may be modest, it will build as the donor ages. These amounts are shown in Table 7–1. The other consideration is that a charitable remainder trust is the only deductible approach that is currently available to assist in the retirement accumulation process.

The client in this example is 45. Because the pension plan is fully funded, the donor can no longer make contributions to it. The spouse is also 45. The anticipated year of death of the surviving spouse is 38 years from the plan's inception. The annual contribution will be $30,000. This will continue until age 65. Between ages 45 and 65, the donor/trustee will direct the money manager to invest the contributions into growth vehicles with little or no income. In the following example, no income is assumed until age 65. The income tax bracket utilized in the example is 38 percent. The estate tax bracket is 55 percent. Table 7–1 compares three different calculation scenarios. The cumulative contribution will amount to $630,000.

TABLE 7–1
Retirement Comparison

	I	II	III
Income payout rate	6%	8%	10%
Growth rate during accumulation phase	10%	10%	12%
Ordinary income rate during payout period	10%	10%	10%
Cumulative income tax deduction	$128,436	$80,080	$51,467
Cumulative net income during life	$1,973,683	$2,177,645	$3,286,530
Endowment to charity	$2,584,587	$2,112,083	$3,798,940
Present value @6% net income & tax deduction	$4,477,728	$469,983	$647,250
Age 45 income tax deduction	$3,415	$1,750	$929
Age 65 income tax deduction	$9,380	$6,553	$4,651

Source: American Renaissance Trust Information Services, version 3.01 © 1992 PhilanthroTec, Inc.

As can be seen in Table 7–1, there are a variety of ways to determine the best combination of payout and deduction percentages. The higher the payout percentage, the lower the income tax deduction. The higher the payout percentage, the higher the annual income, provided that the investments perform at least at the level of growth and income projected. What is also evident is that on a present-value basis, the differences between the first two examples are not great. The difference, however, between the third example and the first two on the same present-value basis is significant. There is a substantial difference in the income tax deductions between each example. When comparing different plan alternatives, quite often the decision is to select the one with the highest current deduction. This may not always be the best course of action. This comparison illustrates that careful consideration has to be given not only to the income tax deduction figures but also to the actual income amounts, both on a current and future basis.

The income tax deduction when the program in Column I accumulates from 11 percent of the contribution in the first year to over 30 percent of the deposit in the final year. As the percentage of payout increases, the percentage of the amount of the deduction decreases. Of the total contributions of $630,000, the cumulative amount deductible in Column I totals $128,436. In Column III, the deduction only reaches a total of $51,467. However, the total net income differential between the two columns is a little over $1,300,000. Clearly the overall economic benefit to the donor in these two comparisons favors the third column.

Each situation has to be measured both on its own merits and against the overall objectives of the donor. If the advisor or a member of the advisory team is making blanket assumptions based upon either preconceived ideas or prior experience with similar situations, they may not always prove exactly applicable to the donor currently experiencing the gift planning process. Each situation has to be judged based upon its own set of circumstances.

Another area that causes major consternation on the part of retirement plan participants who are near or at retirement is the onerous income and estate tax regulations that deal with qualified retirement plan distributions. The rules and regulations that govern the way in which retirement amounts are distributed to plan participants have also gone through major revision over the last two decades. These revisions have not proved favorable to the retiring or terminating, highly compensated retirement plan participant. In fact, at the higher accumulation levels, the combined income and estate tax rates are virtually confiscatory. In order to understand the impact of these changes, it is necessary to review their evolution.

RETIREMENT OPTIONS

At one time, it was not really necessary to retire at any specific age under the rules of qualified plans. It was possible to continue to work and receive contributions to a qualified plan well beyond normal retirement age. Today an employee, even an owner/employee, can continue to work after normal retirement age, and in some cases the company can continue to fund benefits beyond normal retirement age, the participant must start receiving benefits under the plan by April first of the calendar year following the year in which he or she reaches age 70 1/2.[4] This regulation applies whether or not the participant is still actively employed and having a contribution made on his or her behalf. The only exception is an employee who owns less than 5 percent of the business, was 70 1/2 prior to January 1, 1988, and did not retire prior to age 70 1/2.[5]

There are various ways a participant can receive distributions from the retirement plan. Benefits can be received either as a lump sum or under a periodic payment schedule. Any early retirement or termination benefit paid to a participant prior to age 59 1/2 that is not directly transferred to an Individual Retirement Account is subject to income taxation and to a 20 percent mandatory withholding requirement at dispersal.[6] If not transferred within 60 days to an Individual Retirement Account, the distribution is also subject to a premature distribution tax of 10 percent.[7] This penalty tax is not imposed in the event of the death or disability of the plan participant. The vast majority of distributions are taxed at ordinary income rates.[8] An exception to this general rule applies to employees who were 50 before January 1, 1986 and allows them certain options on the treatment of the distribution for tax purposes.;[9]

The onerous section of the regulations pertains to excessive benefit distributions to plan participants. The Internal Revenue Code details these distributions as any aggregate retirement benefit paid to an individual in a calendar year that exceeds $150,000 or $112,500 indexed for inflation from the enactment date of 1986.[10] Once the indexed amount reaches $150,000, it will provide the sole index. This was originally projected to occur in the early 1990s, but that date has been pushed back into the later part of the decade. If the maximum amount is exceeded in any calendar year, in addition to the ordinary income tax due a 15 percent penalty tax is also imposed.[11] There are some grandfathering provisions available for accumulations that are greater than $562,500 on August 1, 1986.[12] These are not automatic and had to be elected by the taxpayer on a tax return filed before 1989. As pension deposits are tax deductible, income taxes are imposed on distribution. Penalty taxes are added where appropriate. Whatever retirement funds are still left in the estate at death are subject to all three taxes: income, penalty, and estate. The total taxes due can amount to over 80 percent of the accumulations.

Another twist added by the pension legislation is the minimum distribution requirements.[13] In order to force moneys out of retirement plans and into the tax system, Congress adopted the minimum distribution rules previously discussed. Many wealthier individuals forestall distribution of their retirement benefits as long as possible. In so doing, quite often they exacerbate the distribution problems. Even when they get to the mandatory distribution age, the only amounts they wish to withdraw are the minimum distribution requirements. Very few retirees want to pay the 15 percent excise tax until absolutely forced to. Many therefore die with large, undistributed pension benefits and pass the problem onto their surviving spouse or to their executors to handle. Unfortunately, when this happens, which is far too often, the magnitude of the situation may be such that the avoidance of the penalty tax is impossible.

One of the other major problems that retirees and their spouses face is the significant misunderstanding and misinformation that abounds in this area among plan sponsors and the advisory community. As there has not until very recently been much dissemination of information about distribution planning, the availability of competent advice is sorely lacking. One major misconception is that the tax issue goes away with the death of the retiree. In fact, if the situation is not properly handled, the tax problem can grow.[14] Many business owners and professionals as well as their advisors are totally unaware of the distribution tax issues. If they are aware, they may be ill-informed. Part of the process of dealing with this issue is competent planning and advice at the time of retirement or distribution. Even if little or no planning is initially done, the tax issues can be addressed and properly provided for by comprehensive planning.

In this planning area, a charitable remainder trust can be of enormous assistance in delaying or negating the impact of the triple tax whammy. It is not possible to name a charitable remainder trust as the beneficiary of a retirement plan distribution and avoid all the taxes due; they must be paid either from the retirement plan assets or from other funds before the gift is made.

This will normally deter any gifts of this nature. Where the charitable remainder trust is most helpful in distribution planning is on a testamentary basis, and a powerful help it can be. The testamentary planning can be enacted by the retiree or the surviving spouse and will take effect at the death of the final party. It is important that the planning be done early on and that all parties involved are well informed about the plan design and the intended outcome. This includes the retiree; the spouse, if any; the heirs; and the estate executors. At the death of the retiree, the surviving spouse is often not able to make rational planning decisions. Without the proper planning, the opportunity to positively affect the distribution process will be lost.

In viewing the following example, the critical focus should be on the after-tax increased income stream for the heirs. In this type of retirement plan distribution scenario, the assets are received at retirement and placed into a rollover Individual Retirement Account (IRA).[15] The surviving spouse is named as the income beneficiary. If there is no surviving spouse, the testamentary charitable remainder unitrust is named as the beneficiary. The income payments from the IRA are received according to a plan selected by the retiree. At the death of the retiree, the surviving spouse receives the remainder of the IRA via a transfer to his or her rollover IRA. The surviving spouse then establishes the testamentary charitable remainder unitrust as the beneficiary. At death, the charitable remainder unitrust receives the entire IRA distribution, and the heirs start receiving income immediately. The enormous increase in net income over the heir's life expectancy will provide quite a legacy for the decedents. Leaving assets to an heir's children can easily be accomplished by the use of life insurance. The increased after-tax income stream can be tapped to provide whatever annual premium dollars are needed.

As can be seen in Table 7–2, the application of a charitable remainder trust into the retirement planning distribution process can produce an enormous lifetime differential in the after-tax spendable income of the heirs. In order to realize this increase, certain steps must be taken during the life of the retiree and spouse. All of the taxes due at the death of the surviving spouse are not negated by the introduction of a charitable remainder unitrust in the role of beneficiary. The excess retirement account excise tax payable is the same in either situation. The estate tax

TABLE 7–2

Assumptions:
Age of spouses - Male 65, Female 60
Age at death of surviving spouse, 75
Heir's life expectancy, 32 years
Income tax bracket, 40%
Estate tax bracket, 55%
Current account balance, $1,500,000
Grandfathered amount, $950,000
Excess Retirement Account at surviving spouse's death, $1,897,600

	Lump Sum	CRUT
Value of pension at death of surviving spouse	$2,993,368	$2,993,368
Excess Retirement Account	284,643	284,643
Excise tax payable on $1,897,620		
Estate tax payable	1,489,799	1,325,210
Income tax payable	601,428	0
Total taxes paid	$2,375,870	$1,609,853
Effective tax rate	79%	54%
Investable for income at 8%	617,498	1,383,515
Heirs' annual income	49,399	110,681
Heirs' increased lifetime net after-tax income	0	1,248,512
Amount to next generation	277,874	0
Charitable donation	0	1,383,515

Source: American Renaissance Trust Information Services, Version 3.01 © 1992
PhilanthroTec, Inc.

is slightly different. The amount included in the estate is the total attributable to the income stream being paid to the next generation. This is included in the estate under "the income to a decedent" regulations. The present value of the income stream is calculated and included in the estate. This is offset somewhat by the deduction in the estate of the remainder interest left to the charitable organization via means of the charitable remainder trust.

With the use of the charitable remainder unitrust, no income taxes are due at the time of death on the lump sum. The inclusion of the present value of the future income stream to the beneficiary is included in the estate for estate tax calculations. Income taxes are paid on the income received by the beneficiary as it is paid out of the charitable remainder trust. The identical tax situation would exist on the income earned from the lump sum from the pension distributed to the beneficiary. The estate and excise taxes must be paid at the settlement of the estate of the surviving spouse. The excess retirement account excise tax would be based upon a revised calculation utilizing the surviving spouse's excess. In order to take advantage of the deferral and sheltering capabilities of the charitable remainder trust, the entire pension proceeds should be gifted. This will require that the taxes attributable to these funds be acquired from another source, such as liquefying other available estate assets. Usually this course of action is not the most economical one. When there are multiple heirs, it may also not be the most equitable.

The preferred method for providing the funding for the taxes is by utilizing life insurance. The proper role of life insurance in this situation can totally satisfy the tax obligation at the death of the surviving spouse. The most economical way of providing the necessary amount would be through the use of second-to-die insurance, payable at the death of the surviving spouse. The premiums can be funded from the retirement plan payments. The need for planning and enacting this process while both spouses are alive is paramount. Waiting to provide the insurance death benefit until the death of the first spouse will prove much more costly or may be impossible to accomplish due to the deteriorating health of the survivor. These reasons alone make early planning paramount.

Provided it is properly invested, the income stream from the charitable remainder unitrust continues for the lives of the heirs. At their deaths, the dispersal of the corpus of the trust is made to the charitable beneficiaries, and the trust ceases to exist. In the appropriate set of circumstances, this planning scenario can provide maximum utilization of the retirement assets for the current as well as the next generation. The key to this strategy's success is the proper utilization of financial and charitable planning. This planning process will involve more than one generation. All parties that will benefit from this strategy should be fully cognizant of the inner workings, the planned results, and their individual responsibilities. Without this coordination, something will surely go awry, and the intended results could turn negative.

Another traditional planning area where the charitable remainder trust can provide additional enhancement is a nonqualified deferred compensation.[16] In virtually every large U.S. corporation and quite a few small ones, some type of deferred compensation is part of the typical executive compensation agreement. These arrangements have become much more popular since the recent legislative curtailments of qualified retirement plans. A nonqualified deferred compensation plan was originally designed as a program in which the corporation promised to pay the executive a percentage or a specified amount of compensation in the future in return for the performance of certain current employment tasks. There was no current recognizable income generated or income tax liability on the part of the employee, and if a contribution was made to a plan by the corporation to fund the future compensation liability, it was not currently deductible by the corporation. It was only taxable to the employee when actually received and only deductible by the corporation when actually paid.

In order to prudently fund for the future compensation obligations and to also allay any fears on the part of the executives as to the funding of these obligations, many corporations make annual nondeductible deposits to a sinking fund account. This account will meet the obligations of the nonqualified deferred compensation plan. As any assets allocated to fund these plans are part of the corporation's assets, they are subject to the claims of the corporation's creditors. In recent years, this has presented quite a problem to a number of executives from various organizations that have merged, been acquired, gone bankrupt, or ceased to exist. As an innovative strategy, the charitable remainder unitrust can be helpful in this situation.

Many executives want to control the deferred compensation funds in order to avoid the problem of these assets or potential assets being subject to the solvency of the corporation. A number of methodologies have been proposed over the years to address this issue. Some have had limited success in dealing with the liability problem, but none have achieved any substantial headway. While all of the deferred compensation plan issues have been developing, a number of changes have occurred involving corporate charitable donations. Over the last decade, corporate donations have maintained a fairly consistent percentage of total charitable contributions in the country.[17] One of the major changes affecting the type of contributions is the desire on the part of many firms to have their employees become more involved in the corporation's charitable endeavors. Melding the nonqualified deferred compensation program with the corporation's charitable interests may accomplish just that.

The mechanics of this arrangement are relatively simple. The conceptual sale must be made to the corporation before it is made to the executive. The basic motivation on the part of the corporation will be to turn a currently nondeductible expense—the contributions to the nonqualified deferred compensation sinking fund—into a current income taxable deposit into a charitable remainder trust. The executive's motivation will be to get control over the assets and not have them subject to the vagaries of the corporation. This can all be accomplished by the executive creating a charitable remainder trust. The charitable remainder trust could favor any organization desired, even the executive's private foundation. The corporation would then make deposits to the charitable remainder trust. These deposits (equivalent to the contribution it would make to the deferred compensation sinking fund) are currently deductible to the corporation.

The contribution is treated as part compensation to the executive and part charitable corporate contribution. The executive is responsible for the income taxes on the increased income. The percentage of the contribution the corporation deducts as compensation to the executive will vary according to the age of the executive and the specifications of the charitable remainder trust. This compensation charge will always amount to the majority of the deposit. In most cases, the executive can meet the increased tax liability from other available funds. This basic concept can be enhanced manifold with the addition of other corporate charitable objectives.

For an executive to participate in this program, the corporation may require that the corporate foundation be one of the remainder beneficiaries of the executive's charitable remainder trust. There could also be a plan design where a portion of the funds allocated to the executive's charitable remainder trust are used to purchase life insurance on the executive's life for the benefit of the charitable remainder trust and in turn the remainder beneficiaries of the charitable trust. Up to 25 percent of the annual deposit can be invested in life insurance premiums. Depending on the plan design and objectives, if the corporate foundation was a remainder beneficiary, a portion of the death benefit would inure to it. This in turn would help to further the objectives of the corporate foundation.

The possibilities of combining this approach with the executive's personal charitable goals and the charitable goals of the corporate foundation can be imaginatively structured to provide meaningful benefits to all parties concerned. This type of solution is certainly not going to work in all situations, yet it can provide interesting alternatives to traditional planning processes to forward-thinking executives and corporations.

Chapter Eight

Hard-to-Value Assets

TANGIBLE PERSONAL PROPERTY

One of the unique features of a charitable remainder trust is the donor's ability to utilize tangible personal property or other hard-to-value assets as the funding vehicle for the charitable gift. This feature provides the donor with significant flexibility in designating assets that can be contributed to a charitable remainder trust. It must be remembered that one of the purposes of a charitable remainder trust is to provide income to the donor. If the asset is not income-producing in its own right, the trust will have to sell it in order to reinvest in a vehicle capable of producing income.

In these gift and sale situations, it is extremely important that all transactions be kept at arm's length.[1] Sometimes it is an extraordinarily difficult decision to donate a tangible personal asset to a charitable trust not knowing whether it will be sold. The requirement to assure that this part of the transaction will not be lost in the event of a tax audit is, however, just that. There can be no prior agreement to sell, either verbal or written. There can be no understandings, no options, no binders, no agreements, nothing that will violate the legitimacy of the transfer of the asset. Anything short of this, on audit, will bring a disallowance of the deduction for income tax purposes. Not only will the deduction be denied, the gift will stand and the donor will no longer have the property and will not be able to receive any income from it.[2]

The list of the different varieties of tangible personal property that may be contributed to a charitable remainder trust is almost as long as the list of all types of tangible property. The types of property dealt with in this chapter include real property, tangible personal property, and hard-to-value intangible personal property. Real property can consist of both land and buildings. The land can be raw or developed. It can be farmland, timber, mineral rights, water rights, or even easement rights. The developed buildings can be fixed or mobile. Land and buildings can be combined in almost any way imaginable. For example, farmland with a house can be donated to a charitable trust. The house can be sold and moved from the property. The farmland can be retained by the charitable remainder trust and rented to tenants to produce income. The property donated can be purely rental, with an excellent income flow and current appreciation. However, a sale of this type of property by the trust may not be in the best interest of either the income beneficiary or the remainderman. The trustees must weigh each situation on its own merits.

Tangible personal property such as art, antiques, collectibles, jewelry, both finished and raw gems, autos, boats, airplanes, computers, and even animals are suitable for donations into charitable remainder trusts. As in the case with real property, the assets do not necessarily have to be sold by the charitable remainder trust in order to produce income. A breeding bull, for example, is a tangible personal asset that may not have to be sold in order to produce income. A valuable painting, on the other hand, will have to be auctioned off in order to provide the necessary investable assets. Gifts of tangible personal property to charitable remainder trusts must either produce income or be sold to produce income. The trust should direct the trustee to dispose of any non-income-producing assets in the year in which they are received. The trustee will also have the total discretion to dispose of any other assets. Restricting any asset to be held for the term of the trust will most likely disqualify it as a charitable remainder trust.[3]

Hard-to-value intangible personal assets comprise a significant part of the wealth of older Americans. These could include such categories as close corporation stocks or bonds, limited market securities, partnership interests, royalty income, or personal notes receivable. Any intangible personal assets that cannot be readily valued would also fit under the general category. Conversion of these often highly appreciated, low-income assets into assets providing significantly higher income is not always a simple matter. Gifting suitable assets from this group into a charitable remainder trust can help to address the income issue.

Charitable contributions of tangible assets require special handling and procedures. They are not as easy to donate as cash or publicly traded securities. A number of charitable organizations are also unwilling to take as charitable donations tangible personal property or other types of nonliquid assets. Quite often, it is not that they do not need or would not appreciate the proceeds from the sale of these assets, but they simply do not have the personnel or the facilities to dispose of the property. In many cases, disposal of the property in an expeditious manner is not readily achieved (e.g., funds are required to pay for upkeep and maintenance of properties). These issues and others like them can deter any charitable organization from readily accepting real property.

In any gift where valuation is required, the services of a third party are needed to provide the absolute independence necessary to remove any question regarding the appraisals done to establish the values of the assets.[4] Allowing a donor to act in the role of trustee for purposes of hiring the appraiser to do the valuation is tantamount to requesting an Internal Revenue Service audit. It is an absolute certainty that the IRS will review the appraisal, and any indication of lack of independence will bring closer scrutiny. The gift of the property is an irrevocable gift; as such, it cannot be retrieved. Problems with the valuation for gifting purposes will not result in the gift being undone, but rather in costly tax problems being created for the donor.

It is essential that the donor interject a third party into the gift transaction. This party's role is to act as an independent trustee, divorced of any influence from the donor. The independent trustee would step in between the donor and the trust and actually receive responsibility for the property in a trust capacity. The independent trustee would contract with the certified appraiser or appraisers to provide for the necessary asset-valuation services. This is normally the first function the independent trustee provides. The next function is the actual sale of the asset. This is a vital step in the process. The independent trustee has the responsibility to assure that the entire transaction maintains a completely arm's length status at all times.

REAL PROPERTY

If it is necessary to sell the asset in order to produce the income needed, the independent trustee would endeavor to do that. Often, the asset is not sold immediately after the appraisal process. This is especially true of real estate and tangible personal property. If funds are needed for maintenance or for proper functioning of the asset, it is the responsibility of the trustee to obtain them. If they cannot be obtained in income received from the trust assets, they must be obtained from other sources, such as possible partial sales of the trust assets, or additional funds being contributed to the trust by the donor. Any donor who gifts assets of this nature to a charitable remainder trust should be cognizant of this additional cash requirement. It is the responsibility of the advisor to adequately prepare the donor for this eventuality prior to the gift transaction.

In this process, the independent trustee assumes the role and the functions of what normally would be that of the regular trustee. Before the independent trustee is engaged, the donor should ascertain the method of compensation for the independent trustee. The independent trustee should also be advised of the management responsibilities that are associated with the property until a sale is accomplished. Provision must be made for the method of payment and the source of funds for such items as property management fees, insurance premiums, utilities and other maintenance expenses. The donor should also review the preliminary appraisal that was obtained by the donor for purposes of estimating the value of the charitable gift. The trustee will determine how the property will be marketed for sale. It is also important to determine who will be the listing agent and whether that will be acceptable to the independent trustee. Once these items have been reviewed and resolved, the gift transaction can proceed.

In the case of real property, the independent trustee's responsibilities commence on the date of transfer of the property. Naturally, a title search will have taken place prior to the actual transfer. The independent trustee should review the title search results with the attorney before assuming title to the property. The deed transferring the title to the trust must be filed with the appropriate governmental unit by the attorney. Now that the property has actually been transferred to the trust, the independent trustee can obtain the necessary appraisal to verify the estimated value of the transferred property. If necessary, hiring a management firm to handle the day-to-day management issues would be the next step. Listing the property with the selected real estate broker and negotiating the sale with the qualified buyer would follow. After the property is sold and the proceeds of the sale are remitted with the attendant documentation, resign as the independent trustee resigns. The trust would then function under the normal trustee arrangement. The funds would be invested by the trustee to produce the desired income results.

There are many issues regarding the property that the donor and the independent trustee have to be cognizant of in order to facilitate the gift as well as the sale. Reviewing each of the more important categories will provide an idea of the scope of the issues that must be resolved in the gifting of real property. Real estate gifts can basically entail almost any kind of property. Real property can be divided into four major sections: residential, commercial, agricultural, and anything else. Residential property can be any type, from single family homes to multiple family residences. Included in this category is raw land that is zoned for residential property. Commercial property is any type of manufacturing facility, retail center, office building, warehouse-type structure, retail business location, hotel or motel, and raw land zoned for commercial use. Agricultural properties include farms, ranches, woodlands, and lakes. The miscellaneous category includes wetlands, mineral or timber properties, or such investments as general, family, or limited real estate partnerships and any other type of property that does not fit into one of the other categories.

ISSUES CURTAILING A SALE

One of the worst scenarios into which a charitable remainder trust can be placed is to be given a property that has severe structural, environmental, or legal issues that could deter or hinder a sale. A complete survey of the property is essential. If the property includes structures, all the questions regarding the condition of the buildings must be reviewed. Often, the structures serve various purposes. For example, the property may contain a motel and a personal residence. Including both of these structures in the same charitable trust may not be doable. The motel is a functioning business with a whole series of independent issues to address, while the personal residence is non-income-producing.

UNSALABLE PROPERTIES

Whether to gift a real property that has no income and little chance of sale due to either the condition of the property or the current market is a question raised quite often by owners and certain advisors. Usually, the approach is to divest the owner of a problem property via means of a deductible charitable gift. Virtually in every instance, the time spent in exploring these types of gifts is not well spent. There are very few proposed gifts of this type that actually provide any benefit to the charity. If a charitable organization does accept a gift of this nature, the ramifications are almost always negative and create significant unforeseen problems.

EASEMENTS

Another of the more important areas to review concerns easements. Can the property be reached by a public road, or does it require easement access through another property? What easements have been granted with the property? Is the condition of all roads and improvements on the property up-to-date and acceptable? What type of utilities and sewerage service the property? Is this adequate to encourage a sale of the property, or do major improvements have to be made prior to a sale?

ZONING

If the property is raw land or partially developed, can it be sub-divided? What, if any, are the zoning requirements for the property? Can the property be built upon? Are there environmental concerns that would preclude selling the property or at least involve costly corrective procedures? Were there ever underground storage tanks on the property, or does it have a history of being used for refuse dumping? Was it previously or is it currently being farmed, mined, or utilized in another fashion? Is this being done by the donor or some other party with previous agreements with the donor? Is the personal residence of the donor part of the gifted property? If so, when does the donor plan on vacating the residence?

MORTGAGES AND LIENS

Once these issues have been addressed, the questions regarding mortgages or liens and the methodology of satisfying any debts before the actual change of title can be delineated. The gifting of property with attendant debt creates tax problems for the donor that can result in substantial income taxes that result from the debt forgiveness being due as a result of the gift.[5] The initial phase of questions can be completed with a thorough review of the prior accounting of the property. If depreciation deductions were part of the economics of the property prior to the consideration of gifting the property, a careful analysis must be done of the past calculation methods in order to avoid any current adverse tax consequences. If they cannot be avoided, informing the donor of the likely outcome of the calculations will be important in order to ascertain whether the gift will still go forward.

These are some of the necessary review steps that need to be taken when a gift of real property to a charitable remainder trust is contemplated. These are not onerous and when assigned to the hands of a professional advisor can be readily accomplished. As this process is developed for a particular property, additional questions peculiar to the piece of real estate will arise and must be addressed. Again, competent professional advisors can ease the entire process. The most important item on their agenda will be the completion of the gift satisfactory to all the involved parties. It is also their charge to advise a donor when the real property will not fit into the parameters of a charitable gift.

PARTIAL INTERESTS

One issue that frequently arises in gifting real property is the gift of a partial interest. How is it to be structured and what will the tax ramifications be? The basic rule is that for gifts of partial interests no deduction will be available for income, estate, or gift taxes unless it is a gift in trust or qualifies under one of the three exceptions.[6] The exceptions are very limited. The basic deduction exception covers a partial interest in a property that represents the donor's entire undivided interest in the property.[7] A remainder interest in a personal farm or residence is also an allowable exemption for deduction purposes.[8] The only other exception is for transfers made exclusively for conservation purposes.[9]

These exemptions can be molded to certain actual situations to provide some degree of flexibility in plan design. The undivided interest rules provide what would appear to be the least amount of flexibility to the donor or to the advisor in plan design, yet in spite of the apparent inflexibility the interpretation of these rules promotes a good degree of planning opportunity. As long as the donor's interest is their 100 percent interest in the property, it can consist basically of any portion of the total property. An undivided interest can exist in the situation where a donor owns a property as a tenant in common with another person. Either donor could give her or his share of the tenancy to a charitable organization as long as the gift consisted of her or his entire share. The new titling of the property would be between the charity and the other cotenant.

An example of an imaginative application of the undivided interest rule could involve the donation of an undivided partial interest in a summer home. A potential donor and spouse use this home only four months out of the year. The rest of the year, they are residents in another state. The home is valued at $500,000 and has no mortgage or liens. The basis in the property is $200,000.

The owners could donate to a charitable organization their entire partial interest in the property for the unused period of the year and take a current charitable income tax deduction for two-thirds of the appraised value. This deduction would amount to $333,000. The two-thirds interest would be conveyed to the charitable organization on a tenants-in-common basis. In such an arrangement, the charity would have exclusive use of the property during each year of their ownership. The charity would also be responsible for the attendant expenses for their portion of the year. A donor who derived this type of tax benefit would most likely donate the charity's portion of these expenses on an annual basis. Other innovative approaches such as this can also be utilized under the regulations.

Virtually all transfers of a portion of spousal joint title property would run afoul of the undivided interest rule.[10] Unless the property were titled as tenants in common and the entire split interest were gifted to the charity, any gift of spousal property would cause disqualification of the gift. A large amount of spousal property is held as tenants in the entirety. In this titling mode, no individual portions can be donated. The same set of circumstances would exist for property owned by spousal couples in community property states.

Probably the most common allowable gifts of partial interest involving real property concern the donation to a charitable organization of the remainder interest in a personal residence or in a farm. This type of gift will qualify for deduction purposes for income, gift, and estate tax. A personal residence is exactly that— the property used by the donor as his or her principal personal residence. Any type of property that would be classified as the donor's personal residence will qualify under this exemption. This includes such diverse properties as vacation homes, mobile homes, yachts, and houseboats.

Another interesting fact is that the gift does not have to be the total property. For example, the gift could consist of part of a farm. The remainder interest in the residence portion of the farm could be gifted and the balance of the property consisting of the tilled land retained. There are a number of ways of arriving at possible divisions in the property before entering into the remainder interest arrangement. Under normal circumstances, the life interest terminates at death of the donor or donors, and the property passes to the remainder charitable beneficiary. There have been cases in which the service has favorably ruled when the remainderman and another life tenant share the remainder interest as tenants in common. The most assured method of guaranteeing the deductions is to keep the transaction as simple and straightforward as possible.

The final exemption for real property is for conservation purposes. In order for the gift to qualify for the deductions, it must be in accordance with the legislation that deems it a "qualified conservation contribution." There are numerous examples of these type of partial interest gifts in virtually every community in America. They can include such diverse charitable gifts as the future development rights for farmland, the preservation of woodlands or wetlands in their natural state, or the preservation of a historically valuable building. All of theses types of charitable gifts will normally involve varying rules and regulations from a number of government bodies, quite often on both a local and national level. Great care should be taken when developing the parameters of these types of gifts to be sure not to run afoul of the diverse rules and regulations of the various parties involved. Competent assistance with conservation gifts is a virtual necessity.

CHARITABLE TRUST-PARTIAL INTEREST GIFTS

If the property that is being considered for a split-interest gift does not fit any of the exceptions, the only available real property, partial interest deduction is for gifts in trust. In fact, this may be the gift method of choice. The only allowable trusts into which split-interest real property gifts can be made are pooled income funds, charitable remainder trusts, and charitable lead trusts.[11] A gift of real estate into a charitable remainder trust will be treated in the same manner as other types of property gifts. Care has to be taken in selecting the type of charitable remainder trust, especially if the real estate asset is going to be retained for any period of time once it has been donated to the charitable remainder trust. Many interesting scenarios can be developed with the gift of a remainder interest in real property to a charitable trust. The adaptability of this planning tool is as varied as the types of property that can be donated.

Charitable gifts of tangible personal property can often present the advisor with interesting planning opportunities. One of the first issues to address is the type of charitable organization that is going to be the recipient of the tangible personal property. In direct gifts, the donation of the property usually develops a current charitable income tax deduction. If the donation is to an organization that is a "like-use" one, whose exempt purpose is related to the property, as paintings are to a museum, the appreciated value can be used as the figure for deduction purposes.[12] If the donee organization's exempt purpose is unrelated to the tangible personal property, the current deduction will be relegated to the cost of the property.[13] If the property is being donated by the creator, the cost basis of the materials used to create the piece is the maximum deductible amount.[14]

FRACTIONAL INTEREST GIFTS

Fractional charitable gifts of tangible personal property are methods that allow a donor to make income taxable donations and yet not give up full possession of the property.[15] Fractional interest charitable gifts of art are excellent examples of this planning methodology. A collector has every intention of donating a painting at death to a museum. This will remove the asset from the estate and free it from being included in the estate for estate tax purposes. No current tax benefits are available from this gift for the donor. The donor lives in New England and spends the entire winter down South. While away, the painting hangs in the principal residence. If the donor gave a fractional interest in the painting to the museum that was ultimately going to receive it, a current income tax deduction for the value of this fractional interest would be available.

The individual donor in this example gives the museum a fractional interest in the painting for three months per year. The painting will hang in the museum during these three months. Whether the museum displays the painting or not is a decision the museum makes. It does not affect the outcome of the gift or the income tax deduction. Annually, the museum receives the painting for display. In the year of the gift, the donor receives an income tax charitable deduction for one-quarter of the appraised value of the painting. As this is a long-term capital gains and "use-related" asset, the deduction is usable up to 30 percent of the donor's adjusted gross income in the year of the gift. If the property is "use unrelated," the deduction would be limited to the basis (cost) of the property and subject to a maximum deduction of 50 percent of the donor's annual contribution base. In this manner, the owner receives a tax deduction that is currently usable and may also receive some personal satisfaction from seeing the painting hanging in the museum. If the arrangement works to the donor's satisfaction, additional fractional interests in this painting or other paintings could be donated to the museum.

CHARITABLE REMAINDER TRUST—INCOME REQUIREMENTS

For all practical purposes, gifts of tangible personal property donated to a charitable trust create no current income tax deduction. In order for the charitable remainder trust to function as intended by the regulations, it must generate income. Each trust is designed to pay the income generated by the underlying trust assets in a percentage payout, depending upon the design of the trust, to the income beneficiary. When a gift of the remainder interest in a non-income-producing tangible personal asset is donated into the trust, this rule is totally violated. It is impossible for an asset of this nature to generate income. Therefore, the charitable remainder trust will be nonfunctional and will be declared invalid.

The only way a tangible personal asset can be gifted into a charitable remainder trust is if it is sold. The donor can direct that any and all non-income-producing assets can be sold at the discretion of the trustee to produce income. A number of attempts have been made to bypass these restrictions. None have produced a viable trust. If any restrictions are placed on the trustee's ability to sell the assets, the validity of the charitable remainder trust will be challenged, and the income tax deductions will be denied. If a donor placed tangible person property into a charitable remainder trust and granted to the surviving spouse life use of the property with ultimate distribution to the charitable organization, the trust would be invalidated as a charitable remainder trust, as the trustee was restricted from disposing of any of the assets to produce income for the income beneficiary.[16]

Other attempts have been made to work around this issue by donating into the trust other capital assets in addition to the tangible personal property asset in order to produce a stream of income. If any restrictions preclude the trustee from selling the assets to reinvest in income-producing property, the charitable remainder trust will be nonfunctional and declared invalid.[17] The only assumption to enter into when gifting personal property assets into a charitable remainder trust is that the trustee will be directed to sell all non-income-producing assets in the year of receipt and will have the discretion to sell any income-producing assets. This must be done in order to produce the needed income.

LIKE USE ORGANIZATIONS

The gift of a tangible personal asset to a charitable remainder trust will quite often be to an organization that does not possess a like use with the property, such as a painting to a hospital. Even if the contribution is made to a like-use charity, such as a painting to a museum, the deduction will be calculated based upon the cost basis, not the fair market value of the assets. Once the numbers are put through the calculation process, the value of the deduction will be virtually nonexistent. The fact that the asset must be sold in order to produce the required income would violate the intent of the like-use regulations. If the trust cannot make use of the property, it will be impossible to qualify for the fair market valuation exception of the like-use rules. The deduction will therefore be based upon the cost basis of the property.[18]

The legal profession has taken a number of differing positions on this issue. Each of these positions has been based upon a varied interpretation of the regulations. To date, every attempt to create a favorable interpretation for a donor has proven unsuccessful. The Internal Revenue Service has been very successful in defining the like-use regulation in the manner described above. In planning gifts of tangible personal property, advisors should fully address with each donor the deduction rules for income tax purposes. In virtually all of the gift situations, the economics of the gift will work regardless of the lack of a significant income tax deduction.

Normally, in these types of gifts, the advisor will be dealing with a non-income-producing, appreciated asset. The creation, via means of the gift to a charitable remainder trust, with this type of asset of a capital gains free sale is in itself a significant economic advantage. The creation of an income stream from a non-income-producing asset is another extremely important economic advantage. Just as in similar situations with other types of assets, there is a need to convert low-yielding assets into higher-income-producing ones. That need often exists with non-income-producing assets as well.

There are innumerable situations where an elderly individual living on a modest, fixed income owns a valuable piece of tangible personal property either acquired earlier in life or inherited from a relative. Selling the property would be beneficial, but because of the taxes due on the appreciation the sale would produce significantly less in income than is often anticipated. The gift of the property into a charitable remainder trust however, would yield a much larger income stream for the donor. Yet this occurs rather infrequently. The main reason charitable gifts are not more prevalent is the lack of knowledge on the part of the advisors and the potential donors.

TANGIBLE PERSONAL PROPERTY GIFT SCENARIO

What happens in many situations is illustrated in the following example. A couple reach retirement age, and they have a painting hanging on their living room wall that was inherited from the husband's uncle Charley 20 years earlier. At the time they inherited the painting, it was modestly valuable. Uncle Charley had brought it with him when he immigrated to the United States. Since then, the artist has died, and his work has become very popular. The couple have no idea that the painting has inflated dramatically in value. They are living on a fixed retirement income and would like to increase their income. They don't know how they can achieve this other than going back to work. No thought has ever been given to selling assets, let alone Uncle Charley's painting.

While waiting at the dentist's office, their daughter is browsing through an art magazine and notices an article about the artist who painted Uncle Charley's painting. She mentions this to her father and suggests he contact the museum mentioned in the article to see if he has something of value. He eventually does, and over the next few months learns that indeed he does own a valuable work. Although just how valuable has not been determined; there has not been a recent sale of this artist's work. The museum puts them into contact with a few appraisers who can provide more insight into the painting's worth. The daughter contacts one of them and has the painting appraised. The appraisal value comes in at $500,000. The daughter suggests that the painting be immediately sold and that the funds be reinvested to produce additional income. The parents are somewhat reluctant. This was a gift from their favorite uncle and is a connection to the homeland of the husband's family. They were, however, looking forward to the increased income possibilities.

While these discussions are percolating, the wife takes a bus trip with a number of her friends, and naturally the conversation gravitates towards Uncle Charley's painting. One of her friends mentions a similar situation that a friend of hers had been in with a very rare book. This friend ended up somehow giving it to her church and in turn receiving income from the church. No one was really sure how that worked, but the arrangement somehow produced more income for this woman than if she had sold the book outright. Upon returning home, the wife tells her husband this story, who also finds it interesting. The daughter continues pushing her parents to sell the painting.

The husband is on the board of the local temple. After a meeting one evening, he mentions his plight with the painting to his rabbi. He also relates the story his wife told him about her friend's friend. The rabbi responds that he has heard of such gift arrangements being made but other than that knows very little about it. He does, however, suggest that the husband contact the planned giving director of the federation of synagogues, as he is well aware of these arrangements. The husband eventually does this, and the full story of a charitable remainder trust is explained to him. The increased annual income stream that would be generated by the gift versus the net yields on an outright sale after paying taxes was calculated by the planned giving director at over $9,000 per year. This represents a 34 percent increase in annual income. The other thing that this gift would accomplish in deference to an outright sale is an eventual return of funds to an organization that had been very helpful to the husband and his family for a number of years. In fact, without their initial help when his grandparents had immigrated to this country the family would have had much more trying times. After a few weeks of discussions, the family decides to enter into a giving arrangement with the temple in return for a lifetime income stream.

The required appraisal of the painting and the drafting of the legal documents necessary for enactment of the trust and the transfer of the property are then completed. Once the organization receives the painting, they can proceed with the sale. This sale can be made directly to a museum or another interested party. The painting can also be sold at auction. Whatever the net sales price, whether higher, lower, or the same as the appraisal price, it will not have an impact on the transfer. This is because the income tax deduction will most likely be nonexistent, as the maximum value that can be used for deduction purposes is the cost basis in the property. The cost basis is the value of the property at the time it was inherited from Uncle Charley. The income stream will be dependent on the net value received from the sale. The net value will be the amount realized after the costs of the sale have been deducted from the sale price. Dependent on the actual value realized from the sale, the income may be higher or lower than the initial projected figures. The situation would be the same if the painting had been sold outright. The cost of the sale must always be deducted from the total proceeds to arrive at the true net amount realized.

The form of charitable remainder trust selected for the couple will be a standard unitrust. In this arrangement, they will receive the same annual percentage income from the principal of the trust regardless of the trust earnings in that year. This type of trust is utilized because increased personal income is the primary concern being addressed. They are also at retirement age, and entering into a trust that has an income stream tied solely to earnings can present concerns. They are also young enough that a standard unitrust will offer them more upside potential as a hedge against inflation than a charitable remainder annuity trust will. However, if an absolutely steady stream of income is essential, the annuity trust will serve that purpose well.

A large number of people in the United States are in a similar position. The assets may not be as readily identifiable as the painting, but they exist. The list of tangible personal assets that can appreciate significantly in value over time is very long. What is needed are knowledgeable individuals and organizations who can enlighten the potential donor and provide for an easy transaction. The key to these gifting arrangements is not only a willing donor but a process that makes the gift and resultant sale smooth.

HARD-TO-VALUE SECURITIES

The final category of hard-to-value assets consists of intangible personal properties represented by various nonpublic securities, investments, debt instruments, and miscellaneous types of tangible personal property. Each of theses assets has its own unique set of issues and problems. Some of these assets are very conducive to gifting into a charitable remainder trust, and some are not that readily adaptable. Any interest that is owned outright by an individual could be suitable for gifting into a charitable remainder trust. Before the decision to gift the asset into a charitable remainder trust is reached, the tax regulations regarding the particular transaction should be carefully scrutinized.

Close corporation stock is an ideal asset for gifting purposes. In a charitable remainder trust, stock that can be converted into income-producing assets is essential. Without this capacity, the gift of close corporation stock will present liquefaction problems for the trustee. Because of the nature of this type of asset, a readily available market for it should be apparent to the trustee. Subchapter S stock, on the other hand, cannot be gifted into a charitable remainder trust, as the trust cannot be a stockholder under current IRS rules.[19] This is not a problem in a regular corporation. For a charitable remainder trust to be an owner of other types of business entities will be dependent on not only the type of entity but also on the type of underlying income.

Except in the right set of circumstances, it is difficult for a charitable remainder trust to make a direct investment or to be a partner in an operating business. The same issues pertain to the trust acting as a limited partner in the majority of real estate partnerships. Most real estate limited partnerships are still debt oriented and concentrate on growth. Neither of these conditions is conducive for a charitable remainder trust. There are some non-debt, income-only, limited partnerships available that may fit as an investment vehicle for charitable remainder trusts. Careful scrutiny of the actual investment in many cases may rule it out.

UNRELATED BUSINESS TAXABLE INCOME

Many investments that may be associated with debt when placed into a charitable remainder trust can create "unrelated business taxable income."[20] Whenever debt-financed property is given into a charitable remainder trust, the tax status of the arrangement must be carefully considered. The result is that in any given year the trust will lose its tax exempt status, and the income received by the trust will be taxable. "Unrelated business taxable income" can arise from other sources, primarily those associated with direct investments in businesses or in publicly traded partnerships. Whenever assets or investments of these types of assets are involved with tax-exempt trusts, the risk of running afoul of the "unrelated business taxable income" regulations is always in the forefront, and unless it can be entirely avoided the risk may not be worth the reward.

This issue is further complicated by the fact that "unrelated business income" does not disqualify a charitable remainder trust from its tax-exempt status forever.[21] This entire area can become very confusing for the unwary. If the income is generated as a normal part of the business activities, it most likely will be "unrelated business income." The problem arises primarily with property that is or has been debt financed. It is sufficient for purposes of this text to alert the reader to the concerns raised by this issue. Proper design and ongoing supervision of the charitable remainder trust can be extremely helpful in alleviating this problem.

When the more esoteric types of assets, such as airplanes, boats, and livestock, are suggested as gifts for charitable remainder trusts, care should be exercised as to the viability of the transaction. Is the property subject to debt? Is there a market where the property can be sold? If the property is not immediately sold after being placed into the trust, how will all costs associated with the maintenance of the asset be paid? Many more questions such as these will arise, depending on the peculiarities of each asset. Absolute care must be taken to assure that the asset donated into the trust can pass scrutiny and not create greater tax problems within the trust than it currently does outside of the charitable remainder trust.

Chapter Nine
Trust-Funding Opportunities

TRUSTEE RESPONSIBILITIES

Once a donor's asset is placed into a charitable remainder trust, the responsibility for the management, investment, and conservation of the property passes into the hands of the trustee. The trustee has a dual fiduciary responsibility. On one hand, the trustee has the responsibility of generating income for the income beneficiary of the trust. On the other hand, the trustee has a responsibility to preserve as much as possible of the trust assets for the charitable remainderman. In fact, for each of these responsibilities, the trustee should also be cognizant of the growth potential of the underlying assets.

One of the trustee's responsibilities is to be totally conversant with the type of charitable remainder trust that is being implemented. The trustee should have a thorough understanding of the inner workings of charitable remainder trusts, with particular emphasis on the individual trust adopted by this donor. The trustee should also be fully aware of the donor's objectives. Without a proper understanding of the objectives of the donor in establishing the trust, actions that the trustee may take in handling the trust assets may be contrary to the overall intention of the donor when the trust was established. The trustee is to act independently of the donor, but if the trustee does not have the interests of the donor in mind, there will be a very unhappy donor. In order to prevent detrimental actions by a trustee, the donor will often reserve the right to replace the trustee.[1]

THE DONOR AS TRUSTEE

In many situations, the donor will also act as the trustee.[2] In some states, there is a need to appoint a cotrustee to avoid having the trust designated as a grantor trust. With the donor acting as his or her own trustee, the issues identified above can be avoided. In any case, whether the donor is the trustee or cotrustee, or another individual or a corporate trustee is selected, the trustee is responsible for investing the assets of the charitable remainder trust to produce the necessary income to comply with the requirements of the trust. The trustee must be well aware of the overall investment and income objectives of the plan. Coordination between the income and investment objectives of the trust is critical to a well-functioning plan.

TRUST INCOME REQUIREMENTS

In a charitable remainder annuity trust and a standard charitable remainder unitrust, the immediate objective is the generation of income sufficient enough to satisfy the income requirements of the trust. In the annuity trust, principal can be used to satisfy the payment to the beneficiary. If sufficient income is not generated to fully satisfy the income needs of the trust, principal must be dissipated.[3] The trustee must be careful not to utilize too much principal, which in turn may cripple the ability of the trust to earn an adequate return. This can set up a situation where the trust principal would be dissipating at a much faster pace than originally anticipated, leading to an early demise of the entire trust.

The situation with a standard unitrust is somewhat different. Like an annuity trust, the standard unitrust requires at least an annual disposition of funds to the income beneficiaries. Rather than being a percentage of the initial contribution, this distribution is based upon a percentage of the account value at the annual evaluation date.[4] If the income in the standard unitrust is not sufficient to fully meet the required income payment amount, a portion of the principal must be withdrawn to fund the deficiency. If the trustee is fully aware of the income objectives and requirements, the investments can be attuned to more properly meet these requirements.

It is quite possible in these two type of trusts to fully meet the withdrawal requirements without ever investing in an income-oriented asset. Since the payments are either a fixed amount each period, as in the annuity trust, or a fixed percentage of the account value, as in the standard unitrust, there is no requirement that income be generated by the investments to meet these objectives. The payments can come from a redemption of a piece of the total account. Most likely, if the account is invested in common stocks, there will be some modest distribution of dividend accumulations. These plus a redemption of a portion of the gain in the investment can make up the required trust distribution. If there is not enough gain in the portfolio to support the balance of the required payment, a segment of the principal must be redeemed to make up the shortfall. With the trustee having a very good understanding of these requirements, intelligent investment decisions can be made that will provide for a well-managed trust.

In order to make an income beneficiary payment in the net income unitrust scenarios, the investment requirements imposed on the trustee concern income. In the net income unitrust, the only way a payment may be made to an income beneficiary is by the underlying trust investments producing income.[5] The income must be earned and credited in the period required in order to qualify for dispersal. Income received after the close of the trust's fiscal year cannot be paid out in the preceding year. In an income-only unitrust, if there is no income earned and received, there are no payments to the income beneficiary. Once the trust fiscal year has closed, the ability of the income beneficiary to receive that equivalent payment is lost forever.

NIMCRUTS

The issue is somewhat different in the case of a net income with makeup unitrust (NIMCRUT). By definition, this charitable remainder unitrust pays out each trust year the net income earned by the trust principal up to the predetermined percentage payout.[6] In years where there is less income generated than required, the differential can be made up in subsequent years when there is excess annual income. In years where there is excess annual income and any previous year's income has been made up, the extra income is added to the trust principal to generate additional future income. Quite often, the challenge for the trustee is to match the income objectives of the donor with the investment allocation and performance of the underlying trust assets.

The trustee has a fiduciary responsibility to both the income beneficiary and the charitable remainderman to invest the principal of the trust in a manner that will provide both parties with the desired results. It is not an easy task to find investments that are going to combine strong income performance with adequate growth potential. Not only should the income beneficiary be interested in receiving the desired income, they should be concerned about the impact of inflation on that income. This will be especially true where the income beneficiary is young and has a long projected life expectancy. If the donor is also the trustee, the awareness of this issue may be even more important. Trying to find the right investments to fit the needs of the particular trust can be challenging.

Another issue that can complicate the investment picture for the trustee is the NIMCRUTs that are designed to pay out income to the beneficiary starting at a certain point in time, such as retirement. In this type of unitrust, the donor's original concept may be to have the funds placed into growth investments until that income is desired and then switch into vehicles that provide an income stream. Many times, this process is much easier to illustrate than to actually put into practice. This is especially true if the donor is also the trustee and as such, has direct contact with the investment advisor. Finding investments that are growth oriented, that have little or no dividend income, and that fully comply with the "prudent man" investment guidelines can prove an interesting challenge to the trustee.

The other task facing the trustee, and in turn the investment advisor, in this type of NIMCRUT occurs in the year where the donor wishes to turn on the income stream and start receiving income. If the trustee has been doing a good job instructing the investment advisor on the correct investment strategy, trust principal is invested in growth-oriented vehicles with little or no income. All or some of these securities must now be sold and placed into income-type instruments. These new investments are not going to yield immediate income. If the investments are in corporate bonds, the income is not immediately received. It is usually received on a quarterly basis. In some bond issues, there may be a delay before interest payments commence. Whatever the peculiarities of the particular investment, income may not be immediately assessable.

This can present possible problems for the income beneficiary and disrupt what might otherwise be a smooth-running trust. All too often, the request to switch the investments from a growth to an income mode comes at the moment the income is needed by the income beneficiary. Actually, it should be done well in advance of that time. This is especially true if the investment is being made into an instrument that pays income on an annual basis. The coordination of the investment objectives with the exact type of charitable remainder trust and the expectations of the income beneficiary are essential to the well-managed trust. One of the essential concepts for all concerned parties to grasp is that the income definition for net income unitrusts is just that— income. The definition includes all forms of income credited to the trust corpus during the trust year. Capital gains are not included as part of the income definition.[7]

This issue can cause consternation on the part of both trustees and donors when they pay little heed to it. Often, before the start of the income period, the donor has forgotten that realized capital gains inflate the value of the trust principal and consequently will inflate the income payments that are in turn payable to the income beneficiary. The donor may be expecting the realized capital gains to be part of the income distribution. It may be difficult for the income beneficiary to accept this explanation, especially when they are looking to the realized capital gains as an income-distribution source. If the donor and the trustee believe this may be an issue in the future, there are basically two ways to address it: One is through trust design; the other is through investment product selection.

TRUST DESIGN STRATEGIES

In a net income with makeup charitable remainder unitrust, the design strategy adopted is dependent on an individual program for each donee. Not only will the objectives of each donee be different, but their ages, their health status, and their investment philosophy will also be different. Each of these components will affect the overall trust design. Normally, with older donors the net income with makeup unitrust is not the design choice. There will not be sufficient time to create a large income pool. There is also, usually, a strong need for immediate income in the trusts designed for older clients. Most often this trust design is utilized with donors who are still, on a personal basis, in an asset accumulation mode. Current income is not the primary motivation.

Health status is also a key component. If a donor has a health condition that affects longevity, the need to create an income fund for use in the future will most likely not be that important. It may, however, be relevant when a spousal income beneficiary is in good health, at a younger age, and has a projected normal life expectancy. This may be especially true where there currently is no need for additional income. Creative evaluation of the circumstances surrounding each donor can lead to innovative solutions in trust design.

Investment philosophy is another key ingredient affecting the design of the trust. If the donor has been an extremely conservative or speculative investor, this basic methodology will carry over into the investment policy of the charitable remainder trust. If the donor acts as the trustee, this will certainly be true. Even if the donor is not the trustee, the trustee will certainly take the philosophy of the donor into consideration in deciding the investment strategy for the trust. Although a trustee is acting completely independently from the donor, the trustee has a fiduciary responsibility to act in the best interests of both the donor and the remainderman. This should be accomplished in a spirit of mutual cooperation. The trustee arrangement should not be adversarial. In most situations, the overall investment philosophy of the donor can be recognized by the trustee.

TRUST FUNDING OPTIONS

The development of the income payout stream from a net income with makeup charitable remainder unitrust can be dramatically assisted in two ways. One is through trust design; the other is through investment product selection. The trust-design solution is used in situations where maximum income potential is desired at some time in the future. As the income payout percentage, once selected, is an irrevocable election, careful consideration of the income needs of the income beneficiary at the point of income receipt is required. Too low of an income payout percentage will have the effect of a potential curtailment of benefits during the income years of the trust; for example, a 6 percent income payout percentage with a 12 percent investment return will result in the loss of significant income to the beneficiary in the early years of the trust. The income stream will grow in the later years, provided the life expectancies of the income beneficiaries are at least of normal duration. This is due to the large trust corpus that will accumulate because of the tax-free accumulations.

Too high of a percentage selection may be unrealistic in light of the potential investment choices available. Too high of a percentage may in effect curtail overall plan benefits because the deductible portion of any contributions are affected by the percentage amount selected for payout. The higher the payout percentage, the lower the deduction. For example, a 12 percent payout percentage with a 6 percent investment return will build up a tremendous "makeup" account that will never be realized unless the long-term investment results dramatically improve.

If the anticipated income earned during the payout period is going to be a relatively high percentage, setting the payout rate at that percentage will allow a higher cash flow to the income beneficiaries. Setting the payout rate at a percentage lower than that which is actually earned will produce a lower income in the early years of the switch to income but depending on the longevity of the income beneficiary can produce a much higher long-term income flow. The complexity of estimating the trends of interest rates in the future led to the development of an innovative funding mechanism for charitable remainder trusts. This funding vehicle is a commercial deferred annuity contract issued by a life insurance company.

Why would a commercial deferred annuity contract be an innovative funding device for a charitable remainder trust, especially a net income with makeup unitrust? Usually, the payments from an annuity contract when received by the annuitant are treated as part return of principal and part interest. The return of principal is treated as a tax-free payment, and the interest is taxed as ordinary income. This same cost-recovery ratio continues for all payments for the life of the annuitant.[8] The tax code states, however, that when a deferred annuity is owned by a nonperson, all payments are taxable as ordinary income.[9] In fact, the income is taxed to the nonperson as it is accrued under the contract. This creates the situation where the deferred annuity is credited with earnings in a particular year. Even though the earnings are deferred under the terms of the annuity contract, they are currently taxable to the owner. Corporations used annuities as one of the major methods of providing internal funding for deferred compensation arrangements. This practice ceased in the 1980s due to changes in the income tax treatment of corporately owned individual annuities, as there was no longer a valid economic reason to own deferred annuities on the lives of any of their employees.

With the advent of this Internal Revenue Code change, an interesting funding opportunity developed for the use of deferred annuities within charitable remainder trusts. In a private letter ruling sought by a taxpayer in a gifting situation to a NIMCRUT using a deferred annuity as the funding vehicle, the Internal Revenue Service ruled that the charitable remainder unitrust is to be treated under the same approach as a nonperson owner.[10] The owner is to be taxed currently on the income of the deferred annuity. The general annuity taxation rules of cost recovery will not apply. The trust, however, is a tax-exempt entity; therefore even though the income is taxable, no taxes are actually paid.

Another important aspect of this ruling is the recognition of what constitutes income under this income-taxation approach. If the IRS had ruled that the cost-recovery method was the income-measuring technique to be utilized, the deferred annuity would not be an appropriate funding vehicle for the NIMCRUT. This would be true because the cost recovery method of allocating part of each payment to principal and part to income would preclude any portion of the principal being paid out under the terms of either the net income (NICRUT) or net income with makeup (NIMCRUT) unitrust. No payout of principal could be made in either type of net income unitrust, as principal is not income. The deferred annuity would therefore not be an appropriate funding vehicle for either type of net income unitrusts under a cost-recovery taxation system. Significantly, however, the IRS did not rule this way.

With the receipt of the private letter ruling delineating that a charitable remainder unitrust is not a "natural person" for purposes of the ownership classification for deferred annuities, the funding horizons for NICRUTs and NIMCRUTs were greatly expanded. When the trustee invests charitable remainder unitrusts assets into capital appreciation investments, any portion of the earnings attributable to appreciation cannot be paid out to the income beneficiary. Only that portion of the earnings that is attributable to income can be paid out to the income recipient. The capital appreciation portion of the earnings must be reinvested by the trustee.

In a NICRUT, this restriction can curtail the use of low-income-yielding appreciating assets. In a NIMCRUT, the makeup provision can be greatly exacerbated by the inability of the trustee to pay out any of the capital appreciation to the income beneficiary. In fact, in a number of situations, the trustees may experience added difficulty finding the correct investment vehicles necessary to provide the maximum available payout of the accumulated makeup amount during the lifetimes of the income beneficiaries. This may be especially true in protracted periods of low-interest earnings.

The other investment issue facing the trustee in the majority of NIMCRUTs concerns conversion at the time the income payouts are needed. In most of these types of trust investment portfolios, the assets will be invested in low- or no-yielding growth vehicles. Converting them in a timely manner to secure high-yielding investments may not be as easily achieved in reality as in a computer illustration. For a variety of reasons, the sale of a particular investment may not be opportune at that particular moment. Some of these reasons may be that the particular investment has a large potential for ongoing capital appreciation; current market conditions have depressed all or a part of the value of the portfolio: or current interest rates are very low, and the potential for sustaining large income payments to the income beneficiaries is nonexistent.

The ability of the trustee to invest the trust assets in a deferred annuity addresses all of the above investment and trust issues. The deferred annuity may be either a fixed (declared interest rate) or variable (nondeclared interest rate) annuity. In virtually every situation, the annuity of choice will be the variable annuity. If one examines the ultimate desired results and the inner workings of a NIMCRUT, the choice of the variable annuity over the fixed annuity becomes obvious. The normal income objective from the donor's point of view is to provide the income beneficiary with the maximum income available at the desired moment it is required or requested. This is to be accomplished by accumulating as much capital as possible during the years when income is not needed. This capital can then be converted to income during the years when income is needed. The deferred fixed annuity does not accomplish both of these objectives in the same fashion or with the same results as the variable annuity.

The deferred fixed annuity will accumulate earnings during the deferral period. These earnings are based upon interest rates that are usually declared on an annual basis. Some issuing companies will guarantee longer interest periods. The interest earned each year will be based upon the cumulative amount of the account from the preceding year. As no withdrawals are normally made during the accumulation phase, the net effect is to create a compound interest deferred annuity. Assuming that the selected payout percentage from the NIMCRUT is the same as the interest credited to the account, as much as the entire income earned by the annuity could theoretically be paid out to the income beneficiary in any one year. In operation, this will seldom be the case, as credited interest rates could be higher or lower than the selected payout percentage. If the credited interest earnings were at least equal to or lower than the selected payout percentage, the lump sum payout of the entire interest account in any one year would be feasible.

The only growth of the corpus of the trust in a deferred fixed annuity will be from income, not from capital appreciation. By its very nature, the deferred fixed annuity cannot have capital appreciation. In the majority of NIMCRUT, a significant period of time will elapse between the initial gift into the trust and the desired year in which income payments to the income beneficiary are to commence. In these situations, the desirability of capital appreciation in the account value will be greatly enhanced. This is where the deferred variable annuity will be substantially different than the deferred fixed annuity. By the very nature of this financial product, capital appreciation investments can be utilized for accumulation purposes. Over time and in the right investment atmosphere, this can provide substantial appreciation in the underlying capital portfolio. The capital appreciation under the annuity taxation rules applied to net income charitable remainder unitrusts could be available for full withdrawal in any one year. The exact amount would be based upon the allowable maximums determined under the net income makeup provisions.

Another major difference between deferred annuities and other possible trust investments is that this investment never needs to be changed during the lifetime of the trust. In net income unitrusts that utilize other investment accumulation products when income is desired, a change in investment vehicles must take place. The accumulation vehicles must be sold and be replaced by income-oriented ones. This can often create an ineffective investment strategy. With the deferred annuity, this does not occur. The same investment product is used for both the accumulation and the payout periods.

During the payout period, there can also be substantial capital appreciation of the underlying investment portfolio. With other types of investments, in order for the trustee to make an income payment to the beneficiary, income must be produced by the underlying portfolio. The deferred annuity, however, does not have to be converted to income-oriented investments. Under the unique annuity taxation rules, income payments can be drawn out of the appreciation account and paid out by the trustee to the income beneficiaries. The generation of actual income is not necessarily required. No other investment opportunity can offer this feature to the trustee. The trustee, therefore, has the option of investing in accumulation-type investments when desirable while still meeting the income requirements of the trust.

Another major feature of trust investments in deferred annuities is the trustee's ability to manipulate income payments to the income beneficiaries based upon their changing needs. With an annuity that is not yet into its annuitization phase, a change in withdrawal amount from each withdrawal period is easily enacted. Withdrawals can be stopped, decelerated, or accelerated at the request of the trustee. These features can add great flexibility to the annual income tax planning of the income beneficiary. The ability to turn the income payments off or on without investing in securities that are too risky for the trust is another added feature of the annuity product.

One final feature of the annuity investment is the ability of the trustee to design the withdrawals to provide a large withdrawal at the death of the first income beneficiary, if desired. This feature can add a good degree of planning flexibility for the income beneficiary. The large or lump sum withdrawal feature of the deferred annuity can add substantially to the flexible approach that the trustee can take to income payments to the income beneficiaries. Special requests with this type of investment vehicle can be easily addressed. No other type of investment can provide this type of adaptability.

The donor and the trustee must be aware that the fees charged by the typical variable annuity company will be higher than those charged on a correspondingly sized investment in a typical mutual fund or managed money account. This differential in charges will range on average from one-half to one and one-half percent annually. This will have an impact on the overall performance of the investment. Naturally, the higher the internal fees charged by the annuity company, the greater the impact on performance. This drain on performance can serve over time to damper the growth of the underlying assets in comparison to other types of investments.

When changes of investment strategy are desired because of market conditions or trust requirements, they can be easily effected under a variable annuity funding scenario. Since all variable annuities use as their investment medium either direct investments into commercially available mutual funds or a mutual fund-type approach with separate account investments, changes in investment policy are instantaneously available. In individual investment portfolios, a change in investment policy can take some time to implement. Extra charges based upon sales of existing holdings and purchase of new ones are avoided. Quite often, these can amount to significant sums. The use of a variable annuity can also dramatically assist in preventing any loss of principal due to changes in investment philosophy or direction.

One of the investment considerations open to the trustee is to mix different investments together. This not only involves different types of investments or different styles within the same investment area, but a mixture of investment structures as well. It may be a prudent investment strategy to place some investment dollars into mutual funds, some into direct purchases, and some into deferred annuities. These investment arrangements can vary, depending on the desired objectives. This ability to commingle investment products does offer additional flexible options to the trustee.

ANNUITY FUNDING SCENARIO

In order to vividly delineate the flexibility of the trust investing in a deferred annuity, let's examine an extended example. Stanley and Myra Orland are both age 40. They have been married for 13 years and have two children, ages 12 and 10. Stanley and his business partner started a business over 10 years ago and 2 years ago went through a public offering of the stock. Prior to this offering, Stanley gifted 200,000 shares of stock to Myra. The cost basis on these shares was 10 cents per share. The current market value of a share is $12.00. The total value of her holdings are $2,400,000. They now hope to diversify this part of the stock investment.

They have the financial obligation of college for their daughters arising in a few years and want to be able to meet the cost of tuition with this asset, and they want to accomplish this objective in the most tax-advantaged way. They also realize that planning for their future retirement is an essential part of an investment strategy. Stanley would love to retire by age 55 or 60 but has been unable to start a retirement plan in the company because of the demands made on profits by the ever-increasing expansion needs of the business. The only retirement vehicle that they have been able to install is a 401(k) plan that does not give to Stanley any significant retirement benefits.

Based upon last year's tax return, Stanley and Myra have an adjusted gross income of $350,000. They do not have a large investment portfolio other than the stock in the business. In order to accomplish their goals, the Orlands have reviewed a variety of options and with the help of their attorney have settled on the idea of creating a $1,000,000 charitable remainder unitrust as the most advantageous way to diversify their investment portfolio. They have thoroughly reviewed the financial ramifications of this decision and have come to the conclusion that it makes tremendous economic sense for them. Future gifting of the asset to a charitable organization is not a problem for them, as the plan is designed to replace the asset in a wealth-replacement trust for their children. One of the critical pieces in the decision-making process was the investment options available to the Orlands within the charitable trust.

The financial advisor recommended by the attorney shows them what impact on their overall plan a variable annuity would have as the funding apparatus for the charitable remainder trust. As current income is not a consideration, the trust of choice would be a net income with makeup charitable remainder unitrust. Funding this trust with a variable annuity would provide an incredible array of flexibility to the overall operational phase of the plan. As the Orlands are only 40, the income tax deduction for the charitable gift will not play an important role in the overall plan. The actual projection of the plan's operational phase appears in Table 9–1.

As Table 9–1 indicates, the income tax deduction is very modest. There are two reasons for this. The first is that the Orlands are quite young. Their life expectancies at age 40 are significant. The other reason is that the withdrawal rate selected was 8 percent. The higher the withdrawal rate, the lower the deduction created. If the withdrawal rate had been lower, the deduction would have been higher. The purpose of creating this charitable remainder trust was not oriented around the income tax deduction.

TABLE 9–1

	I Gift	*II* Gift	*III* Gift
Gift	$1,000,000	$1,000,000	$1,000,000
Income tax deduction	$40,250	$40,250	$40,250
Retirement age	55	60	65
Annual income withdrawals for college	$25,000	$25,000	$25,000
Annual retirement income for both spouses	$219,931	$323,150	$474,814
Additional maximum withdrawal at age 65	$1,830,282	$3,158,613	$5,110,367
Assumed rate of return: 8%			
Assumed payout rate: 8%			

Source: American Renaissance Trust Information Services Version 3.01 © 1992 PhilanthroTec, Inc.

Three different retirement ages are illustrated in Table 9–1. These three were selected to provide a finite comparison of the value of delaying the receipt of any proceeds other than the withdrawals for education expenses to retirement at age 65. These comparisons will shed some light on the best approach to this question. It should be remembered that there are two parts to the mathematical answer to this question: the amount of the annual income stream, and the amount of the withdrawal available from the trust in addition to the annual sums. In addition to the actual dollar amounts, there will exist in each situation a number of other personal issues that will affect the withdrawal results.

One of the Orlands' objectives is to provide for the educational needs of their two children from the withdrawals from the charitable remainder trust. Since the annuity investment easily allows for the start and stop of the income stream, it facilitates ease of withdrawals. As long as there have been earnings and growth in the investment, withdrawals sufficient to meet these needs can be easily facilitated. In this example, annual expenditures of $25,000 have been calculated for each child for a four-year period. This will equal a total withdrawal of $200,000. There are sufficient funds based upon a net 8 percent return to meet the illustrated amount. If larger or extended withdrawals were needed, these could also be addressed.

In gross dollars, the value of delaying retirement from age 55 to age 65 is significant, more than doubling the annual withdrawal. In present value figures, the difference, however, is negligible. Delaying the actual receipt of the dollars by 5 or 10 years does not have a material impact on the present value of the income stream. The present value of the lifelong income stream at a 6 percent interest discount starting at age 55 is $1,433,778. Based upon the same calculation, the present value of the lifetime income stream at age 60 is $1,433,753 and at age 65 is $1,399,426.

Starting the withdrawals at age 55 does represent a larger present value return to the Orlands. The differential in present dollars between the lowest and the highest numbers is less than 3 percent. With the same parameters, when the maximum lump sum available is withdrawn at age 65, the results on a present-value basis are not as different as would be imagined. In Table 9–1, the maximum withdrawals available at the illustrated age of 65 range from $1,830,282 to $5,110,367. On a present-value basis, using a 6 percent discount, the largest amount received would be by deferring all receipt of funds until age 65. The lower present value amount would be produced by the withdrawals beginning at age 55. The difference between these two present value totals is less than 6 percent, or under $80,000.

The income in all three comparisons is designed to continue over both Stanley's and Myra's life expectancies. Currently, that is actuarially estimated to be a total of 43 years. If either or both of them live longer than this estimate, there would be, based upon the illustrated amounts, sufficient dollars available to continue the income stream for as long as necessary. In the event that one or both of them ever required nursing home assistance, the dollars necessary to fund these expenses would be available.

One of the most interesting features of the deferred annuity funding is the absolute flexibility that is put into the hands of the trustee to vary the income withdrawals for the income beneficiary. Based upon the funds available, almost an infinite number of income payment patterns can be arranged. The Orlands will be able to vary the income payments at any time and at any interval. In actual practice, the number of adjustments to the payment stream will normally not occur that often.

No matter what the funding method used by the trustee, the primary investment concern is the fiduciary responsibility that the trustee bears to both the income and remainder beneficiaries. The investments must be made in a prudent manner to protect the principal for the ultimate distribution to the remainder beneficiary. The trustee must wear two hats: On one hand, the responsibility is to generate the necessary income for the income beneficiary; on the other hand, the shepherding of the principal for the remainderman is a primary interest. Sometimes, balancing these two in a particular investment strategy can prove very challenging.

Chapter Ten

Life Insurance and Wealth Replacement Trusts

LIFE INSURANCE AS A CHARITABLE GIFT

Life insurance can by itself be a worthwhile asset to donate directly to a charitable organization. This outright donation can quite often lead to substantial income tax deductions. Both existing contracts and new contracts can be used as charitable gifts. Any existing life insurance contract can be utilized, whether it is paid up or not. A brand-new policy taken out expressly for gifting to a charity, with a charity or a charitable trust directly named as the owner and beneficiary of the policy from date of inception, also makes a viable deductible gift.[1]

Merely naming a charitable organization or a charitable trust as the beneficiary of a life insurance policy does not by itself create a deduction for income tax purposes.[2] The donor still is the owner of the contract and retains all the attendant rights of ownership. At the time of the insured's death, the death benefit of the policy is included in the estate. There is an offsetting estate tax deduction for the amount of the death benefit gifted to the charitable entity at that time. In order for a deduction to be available for income tax purposes, the ownership of the policy must be changed to the charitable entity.

The gift of a life insurance policy to a charitable organization or charitable trust represents the opportunity for the donor to dramatically leverage the impact of the amount of their gift due to the death benefit of the contract. Life insurance proceeds payable to a charity will dramatically exceed the cumulative premiums paid and ultimately result in a significantly higher contribution to the organization or trust.

The income tax deduction that can be recognized in the case of an existing life insurance contract will be for the replacement value of the paid-up policy.[3] For a policy that has an existing cash value, the deduction will be for the value of the policy.[4] Subsequent annual deductions will be available for the ongoing annual premiums. When the policy is a brand-new one, the maximum available deduction will be for an amount equal to the annual premium payment.[5]

All of these deductions are limited to the maximum amounts available under the deductibility rules. Existing policies are further limited to the cost basis of the contract for deductibility purposes. The cost basis is defined as the total of all premiums paid. If the cash value of the contract exceeds the premiums paid, the deduction is limited to the cost basis. Since the increase in cash value over the premiums paid would be taxed to the owner, upon surrender of the contract as ordinary income this amount must be reduced from the cash value to create a deduction equal to the cumulative premiums paid. Life insurance policies fall under the reduction rules for charitable gifts of ordinary income property. If the cash values do not exceed the premiums paid at the time of transfer to the charity or the charitable trust, the deduction is calculated based upon replacement value of the policy, which will slightly exceed the cash value of the policy.

One particular issue that all donors of life insurance should initially check before gifting a policy, either existing or new, is the appropriate state law regarding the rules on insurable interest. Some states have regulations stating that an individual or entity that does not possess an insurable interest in the person being insured cannot be the owner, applicant, or beneficiary of a life insurance policy on that person's life. In a private letter ruling, the IRS used such a state law as a means of denying the charitable deduction for a life insurance premium.[6] A number of states that had like laws such as the one cited in the private letter ruling have taken steps to address this issue. Some have been successful, and some have not. It is clearly advisable for any donor contemplating a gift of a life insurance policy to a charity or a charitable trust to have legal counsel thoroughly research the applicable state law on this issue.

LIFE INSURANCE IN CHARITABLE REMAINDER TRUSTS

The use of life insurance in conjunction with charitable remainder trusts is accomplished in two fashions: within the trust itself or outside the trust. The funding of life insurance within the charitable trust is done from either direct contributions to the trust or from the earnings of the trust assets. The funding of the life insurance outside the charitable trust is normally done with annual noncharitable gifts made into a wealth replacement trust.

The primary reason for the gift or the direct purchase of a life insurance policy in a charitable remainder trust is to enhance the remainder amount to the charitable organization. The death benefit from a policy on the life of a donor can add significantly to the remainder interest. To some donors, this can be an added incentive for instituting a charitable remainder trust. The IRS has ruled that life insurance can be used as a charitable remainder trust investment.[7] When utilizing life insurance in such a trust there are practical considerations that will affect the amount of the premium contribution.

It must be remembered that the life insurance is being placed in a charitable remainder trust, which by definition is designed to provide income to an income beneficiary. Sufficient other assets must be in the trust to produce the income required by the trust specifications. If the trustee borrows from the life insurance policy to invest in income-producing assets, the problem of acquisition indebtedness will surface.[8] This will result in unrelated business income but not unrelated business taxable income. It is certainly advisable not to create a charitable remainder trust scenario with one of the investment criteria being borrowing from cash values for reinvesting in income-producing assets.

Use of life insurance to enhance the charitable remainder is not that common. More often, the use of life insurance that is observed within the auspices of a charitable remainder trust is in the net income with makeup unitrust. Here, the objective is not to necessarily increase the remainder interest, although that does ultimately happen, but rather to increase the principal of the trust at the death of the first income beneficiary to die, in order to enhance the subsequent income to the remaining beneficiary. This technique can work quite effectively in a net income with makeup unitrust where annual deposits are being made in order to accumulate a sum for income payments at some point in the future.

In a net income with makeup charitable remainder unitrust, the normal objective is to accumulate as much capital as possible within the trust during the period of time that income is not needed, in order to pay out maximum income at a point in the future. In annual contribution net income with makeup unitrusts, any disruption in the contribution flow will have adverse consequences on the principal accumulation and in turn on the income flow. A major interruption of annual contributions would be the death of the donor primarily responsible for the making the gift. A cessation of contributions at that point could have a dramatic impact on a financial plan.

Insuring against the death of the donor, would be a logical investment of the trust. Not only would the remaining income beneficiary clearly benefit from a larger income stream, but the remainderman would receive an increased amount, from the principal of the trust at the death of the last income beneficiary. The IRS has not issued any rules on the percentage of the contribution that can be allocated in a net income unitrust. There have been suggestions that the life insurance should be incidental to the total contribution. In a qualified defined contribution pension plan, life insurance, incidental to the plan, is defined as a premium amount less than 50 percent of the annual deposit.[9] The IRS suggests using an amount that is a maximum of 50 percent of this percentage for charitable remainder trusts. Therefore, the maximum amount that should be allocated to life insurance premiums is 25 percent of the annual contribution to the charitable trust. The following is an example.

PENSION PLAN SUPPLEMENT

Shirley Blackman is a very successful orthodontist who has been in practice for a number of years. She is currently 45. Her husband is a corporate attorney and is 40. Shirley has been contributing the maximum amount to her pension plan since she started in her practice 20 years ago. Her accountant has advised her that she will have to start curtailing contributions on her own behalf, as the pension plan will soon be approaching the maximum funding limitations prescribed by law. Shirley wants to build up a larger retirement amount to supplement her pension. The accountant is cognizant of how involved Shirley is with the dental school that she attended and suggests she consider using a charitable remainder trust favoring the school as the accumulation vehicle. He brings in a charitable gift specialist to thoroughly review the unique features of the net income with makeup unitrust with Shirley and David. Both advisors emphasize how such a program can emulate a pension plan.

As Shirley is the major wage earner in the family, she has exercised the provision in the pension plan that allows for the allocation of a portion of the contribution to a life insurance policy to guarantee that a sizable asset will be available for David in the event of her early death. She asks the accountant and the advisor if something like this can be arranged in the charitable remainder trust. She is assured that it can. After careful consideration, a net income with makeup charitable remainder unitrust is established. The annual contribution that Shirley will strive to gift into the trust is $30,000. Assuming that her practice continues to generate income at the current level, this amount should not be burdensome. The annual gift is not mandatory, but based upon the desired accumulation that Shirley wishes to have at retirement in 20 years, it is a desired gifting level. In order to offer some guarantee to David that trust capital will be available for income in the event of Shirley's death prior to retirement, 25 percent of the annual gift is allocated to the purchase of life insurance on her life. This will represent a $7,500 premium annually invested into a life insurance contract on Shirley's life. This will provide an initial death benefit of $377,339.[10]

Annually, Shirley will gift $30,000 into the charitable trust, which will be allocated by the trustee into both a life insurance premium and an investment account. The projected value of the account at Shirley's retirement age of 65 will be $1,402,758. Had the insurance not been purchased with part of the annual gift the value of the accumulation at the same age would be $1,482,687. The differential in accumulation is the cost of the life insurance protection. The present value of the annual differential in

income, at 6 percent, is $1,993 per year. This is the true differ-
ential cost. The policy premiums will continue until normal retirement, at which time either annual dividends or internal
policy values will be used to pay the annual premiums.

Seven years after starting the gifting program, Shirley suffers
a severe stroke. She dies from complications of the stroke about
six months later. At that time, the charitable remainder trust has
accumulated at an 8 percent return a total account value of
$216,823. To this, the trustee can now add the death benefit,
which in the seventh year would have grown to $389,000[11], and
invest the assets into income-producing ones to provide an
annual income for David. If the life insurance had not been purchased, the $30,000 annual deposits would accumulate at the
same investment rate to a total of $289,098. Based upon an 8 per-
cent trust payout rate, the annual income in that scenario would
be $23,126 instead of the $48,466 generated by the trust containing the life insurance death benefit. In this situation, there
would be an initial period during the first few years where
the makeup provision would increase the income payments
to David.

As can be seen from the above example, the life insurance in
an early death scenario can be extremely beneficial to the remaining income beneficiary, but it can also be beneficial to the
charitable remainderman. The remainder benefit, assuming that
it does not grow or shrink between the time of Shirley's death
and David's death, will be $605,823 when the life insurance ben-
efit is combined with the investment account. This compares
with the $289,098 remainder benefit if no life insurance had been
purchased. Each donor, based upon their own individual situations, can weigh the merits of purchasing life insurance.

There is another instance where the purchase of life insurance
with part of the contribution may be a viable alternative. This
takes place in those instances where the donor desires to enhance
the remainder benefit over and above the amount of the accumulated trust investments. Life insurance serves as the only instrument that can be significantly leveraged to add substantially
increased amounts to the remainder benefit at reduced costs. This
does not occur that often, but some donors with specific charitable objectives in mind may utilize this technique.

WEALTH REPLACEMENT TRUSTS

Once property is gifted to a charitable organization or a charitable trust, the asset is no longer in the estate of the donor. Being out of the estate also means that it can no longer be left to or utilized by the heirs. One of the major stumbling blocks with many potential charitable donors completing charitable remainder trusts is the realization that their children are not going to receive the assets gifted into the trust at their death. In order to address this issue, the concept of the wealth replacement trust was developed.

A wealth replacement trust is not a charitable trust. Like the charitable remainder trust, the wealth replacement trust is an irrevocable trust.[12] It is often used by charitable donors in conjunction with their gift of a large asset to a charitable organization. The purpose of the wealth replacement trust is to replace the value of an asset gifted to a charitable entity to the donors' selected heirs, usually their children. The wealth replacement trust is usually funded with annual gifts that are utilized by the trustee to purchase life insurance on the life of the donor or the donor and spouse. The face amount of the life insurance contract can be for any amount but usually bears some relationship to the value of the property gifted to the charitable entity.

Not every charitable remainder trust requires or needs a wealth replacement established in conjunction with it. A thorough examination of the entire estate asset picture along with a full discussion with the donors of the desired asset distribution plan for their heirs is necessary in order to establish the need or desire for replacement of the donated assets. Even then, if the children are adults, they can own the life insurance on the lives of the donors outright. There may be more than enough assets in the estate to satisfy the desires of the donors as to the distribution plan of their assets.

A wealth replacement trust is an irrevocable life insurance trust. If it does not already exist, the donor or donors create a separate living irrevocable life insurance trust in addition to the charitable remainder trust. An independent trustee is selected, not the donor or the spouse or anyone considered controlled by them. Since this trust is irrevocable, assets placed into it are outside the estate of the donors. The normal beneficiaries of the wealth replacement trust are the child or children of the donors.

The wealth replacement trust would operate in conjunction with the charitable remainder trust to provide the desired outcome of the estate plan. As was previously examined in the zero estate tax illustration (Figure 5–1), the wealth replacement trust provides the instrument to shelter the capital equivalent to the desired amount of estate assets from all estate taxes. The funding for the gift into the wealth replacement trust is normally initially provided by income tax savings generated by the charitable gift deduction. The ongoing funding is received from an allocation of a portion of the increased income flow to the income beneficiaries. This is normally generated from the reinvestment of the donated charitable trust assets into higher income-producing investments.

The life insurance policy usually used in the wealth replacement trust is a survivorship or a second-to-die policy. If a second-to-die policy is not the life insurance of choice, a first-to-die or single life policy can be utilized. With many individuals having longer life expectancies, the possibility of one of the spouses living longer than anticipated by the mortality charts is not that remote. If this does take place, the availability of the proceeds of a life insurance policy payable for the benefit of the children on the life of the first spouse to die would be the equivalent of passing all or a portion of the estate assets to the next generation while one of the asset owners is still alive.

One of the circumstances that may present an issue for the donors is qualifying the annual premium deposits to the wealth replacement trust as gifts of present interest. The severity of this problem will depend on the amount of the premium for the life insurance policy, the number of beneficiaries of the wealth replacement trust, or other gifting options currently being exercised by the donors. Qualifying the yearly premiums under the annual gift tax exclusion is an important consideration in order to guarantee that the death proceeds payable to the wealth replacement trust will pass free of all taxes. If this cannot be accomplished in a direct fashion, finding a means to qualify the premiums under the annual gift tax exclusion will be a paramount consideration.

It is important to recognize that the relationship between the income tax deduction and the increased annual income associated with a charitable remainder trust, and the life insurance premiums gifted into the wealth replacement trust is imputed and not direct. The funding for the wealth replacement trust can come from a number of sources available to the donor. Also, the insurance used within the wealth replacement trust can be provided from various sources. As previously mentioned, the life insurance can be on either both or one of the spouses. The methodologies of providing the required amount of premium dollars to qualify under the annual exclusion gift tax rules can result in several ownership patterns.

LIFE INSURANCE SPLIT OWNERSHIP

In addition to the traditional direct ownership of the entire life insurance policy by the wealth replacement trust, other arrangements would involve some form of split ownership of the life insurance policy. Considering a split-ownership arrangement would be important if the annual life insurance premiums exceed the available annual gift tax exclusions, or for some other reason these were not available. The donors may have other purposes for the annual exclusions. It should be noted that the lifetime exemptions of each donor could be utilized to qualify the premiums as current interest gifts. This methodology should normally be used only when the other available alternatives cannot be.

The mechanism used in which the life insurance premium and death benefit would be split is a split-dollar life insurance program. Life insurance can be designed and purchased on a split-ownership basis.[13] The ownership and death benefit can be split between two or more parties. Usually, it is a two-party split arrangement. The major reason that a split-dollar life insurance plan may be the plan of choice is to help develop a manageable gift amount for the life insurance, payable to the wealth replacement trust. The classic use of split-dollar premiums and death benefit is between the employer and the employee. The employer contributes the lion's share of the premium for the cash values accruing to the policy, and the employee contributes the cost of the pure death benefit. This cost is equivalent to the cost of term insurance for the age and face amount of the party being insured. The death benefit provided for the employer is the cumulative value of premiums paid. The employee's beneficiary receives the balance of the face amount. In the wealth replacement context, the beneficiary will be the wealth replacement trust.

The amount of the measurable gift to the wealth replacement trust is this equivalent annual term premium for the yearly death benefit. This amount will always be a percentage of the total permanent premium. The older the insured, the higher the allocation of that portion of the premium attributable to the term insurance. A procedure for utilizing the irrevocable wealth replacement trust in the split-dollar arrangement must be followed to assure that the death proceeds will be outside the estate of the insured party. Not precisely following these steps will most likely result in the inclusion of the life insurance proceeds in the estate of the decedent. Competent professional life insurance assistance in this matter is essential.

If the employer is unwilling to enter into a split-dollar arrangement with the employee or if there is no employee-employer relationship, split-dollar funding of the wealth replacement trust can still be effected. The split-dollar agreement would be between individuals rather than with the employer. The usual parties to this arrangement would be the donor of the charitable trust and the spouse. The donor would be responsible for the bulk permanent portion of the premium and would in turn be entitled to a death benefit equal to the cumulative premiums. The spouse would be responsible for paying the part of the premium based on the term insurance costs on the balance of the death benefit. This amount would be gifted by the spouse into the wealth replacement trust each year to maintain that portion of the death benefit.

This would represent the amount of the measurable gift each year to the wealth replacement trust for gift tax reporting purposes. The wealth replacement trust would have the premium payment responsibility to the insurance company for the death benefit in excess of the cumulative premiums portion of the death benefit. Upon the death of the insured donor, the donor's estate would receive a death benefit equal to the cumulative premiums paid by the donor, and the wealth replacement trust would receive the balance of the death benefit. As in the situation with the employer-employee, split-dollar plan, exact rules and procedures must be followed to guarantee the viability of this technique. The assistance of a competent life insurance professional is also essential.

When a charitable remainder trust and a wealth replacement trust are properly used in conjunction with each other, the rewards to the donor or donors can be very meaningful. As has been previously demonstrated in the zero estate tax approach, it is possible to totally eliminate all estate taxes with the proper implementation of a variety of trust-planning techniques. In those situations where there are sufficient assets that require utilization of sophisticated estate-planning methods, the outcome can be very meaningful. The results will vary depending on the circumstances, but the majority of situations can be summarized in the following manner.

In a number of potential charitable gift situations, the loss of the asset to the heirs can present a major stumbling block to the completion of the gift. Replacement of the asset with life insurance, within the estate only, will serve to increase the estate and result in higher estate taxes. Gifting of assets directly to the heirs has been severely curtailed by the combined gift and estate tax regulations. The only major relief that is available is to create an asset outside the estate of the decedent that will replace the value of the assets gifted to the charitable remainder trust. Without the ability to create the capital within the wealth replacement trust in a cost- and tax-efficient manner, the overall charitable gift and estate plan will be in jeopardy. Therefore, in many potential estate and charitable gifting situations, the proper coordination of the charitable gift planning with wealth replacement is critical to the successful completion of the charitable gift itself.

Chapter Eleven

Charitable Remainder Beneficiaries

SELECTING REMAINDER BENEFICIARIES

Selecting the proper remainder beneficiary for a charitable remainder annuity trust or unitrust is one of the most important decisions that the donor or donors of the charitable trust must make. Many donors have no question about which charitable entity is going to be the recipient of the remainder interest. One of the donor's motivating factors in the establishment of the charitable remainder trust may have been an interest in a particular charity or cause. Other donors may have a very difficult time deciding on a particular organization and may wish to reserve the actual selection process for a later date. The key to any selection is careful consideration not only of the various qualification rules but the consequences of a particular choice.

Not only is the remainder choice of a charitable entity important, the income, gift, and estate tax ramifications of certain choices can vary dramatically. It is important to fully understand all sides of the issues regarding a particular selection. Once the required income payments have reached their termination, either at the death of the final income beneficiary or the expiration of a certain term, the remainder interest must be transferred by the trustee to the qualifying charitable entity or retained by the trust for the use of that entity.

In Chapters Two, Three, and Four the various tax code categories of charitable entities were discussed. The tax code has set an organization described in Internal Revenue Code Section 170(a) as the minimum definition for the remainder interest in a

charitable trust. That code section details those types of charitable organizations that satisfy the requirements allowing
income tax deductible gifts to be made to them. These requirements set the stage for the minimum allowable charitable trust
remainder beneficiary designation. In actual application, this
would allow the donor to pass the responsibility of naming a remainder beneficiary or beneficiaries to the trustee of the charitable trust.

In following this minimum requirement, however, the donor
has created qualification issues for income, gift, and estate tax
deduction purposes. Not all organizations described in this code
section will qualify for the 50 percent income tax deduction.
Some may not be eligible for a gift tax deduction. A number will
also not qualify for an estate tax deduction. An organization may
qualify under one set of deductibility rules and not another. It
therefore becomes impossible to determine at what percentage
the gift to the charitable remainder trust is deductible and if it
qualifies under gift and estate tax deduction regulations. In order
to properly address these issues, it is paramount that the donor
establish the tax status under all three taxation systems of the
selected remainder beneficiary.[1]

Tax regulations also require that provisions be made within
the governing charitable remainder trust document for alternative remainder beneficiaries.[2] One can see why this is an important provision. In many instances, the remainder beneficiary will
not be receiving any funds for a number of years. In some situations, it can be quite a number of years. What happens to the
trust proceeds if the named charitable remainder beneficiary is
no longer in existence at the time the trustee is required to disperse the trust principal? Without the proper guidance within the
trust document, the trustee will be unable to transfer the trust
principal to any organization. The matter will have to be resolved
by petitioning the court for proper guidance.

The Internal Revenue Service's position is to deny the tax deductions in this set of circumstances.[3] The reasoning is that the
court, lacking any specific instructions within the trust document, is free to name any organization as a recipient of the trust
principal and in so doing could name one that does not fit under

the statute as a qualified charitable organization.[4] For this reason, it is paramount that the donor select an alternative remainderman and the trust document contain specific language to allow for this or alternative selections. The language should be specific enough to qualify the alternative remainderman under the 50 percent income tax deduction.[5]

Trust language also plays an important role when the charitable remainder beneficiary selected by the donor is not designated as an irrevocable beneficiary.[6] The donor has the option of naming the charitable remainder beneficiary as either irrevocable or revocable. In fact, irrevocability may even be assigned on a proportional basis.[7] By retaining the right to change or alter the remainder beneficiary, the donor can create tax deductibility issues. Proper trust wording is essential to assure that the deductibility of the gift is not lost with the allowance of this flexibility.

There is no requirement that the remainder interest be just one charitable organization. There may be multiple remainder beneficiaries. The trust document must allow for this possibility and provide the appropriate language. These provisions are necessary to guarantee that this flexibility will not jeopardize the charitable deduction in the three tax code areas. By allowing not only for multiple remainder beneficiaries but also the ability to change any and all of these, the trust increases the responsibility of the donor and trustee to select charitable entities that properly qualify under all three tax code provisions.[8] At no time should the charitable trust deductions be put in jeopardy due to improper selection of a remainder beneficiary.

As was reviewed in earlier chapters, there are basically two types of charitable organizations that qualify under the various sections of the tax code as remainder interest beneficiaries in charitable remainder trusts: public charities and private foundations. There is also a category of foundation that has some of the characteristics of both a public charity and a private foundation.[9] This charitable entity is known as a *community foundation*. The selection of the type of charitable entity as the remainder interest will determine the percentage limitation of the adjusted gross income that can be used for income tax deduction purposes. These qualification rules were detailed in Chapter Three. The deduction for both gift and estate tax purposes is not affected by the type of charitable remainder beneficiary selected.

In selecting a public charity, the removal of any question of the income tax deductibility is as easy to verify as looking up the organization's name in the Internal Revenue Service directory of charitable organizations. For the most part, the listing of an organization in this publication will also verify the deductibility of the charitable gift for gift and estate tax purposes. The service updates the listings on a periodic basis. These listings, as previously discussed, are contained in the IRS "Blue Book." If for some reason an organization is dropped from the listing, contributions made up until the announcement will remain deductible. Contributions made after that date will be disallowed as a deductible item for all three tax areas.[10]

A charitable organization could not be listed in the publication for a variety of reasons. It, for example, could have had a name change or come into existence after the publication date of the latest list. Even so, if an organization is not listed in the publication, a donor can easily verify the organization's qualification by requesting a copy of their determination letter from the IRS.

If the donor does not wish to name a public charity as the remainder interest beneficiary in the charitable trust, the other possible choice is a private foundation. As previously discussed, it is very important that the donor designate a charitable entity as the remainder beneficiary. The donor may select the private foundation as the remainder interest beneficiary for a variety of reasons, which will vary based upon each donor's wishes, concerns, and objectives. In many cases, the charitable objectives of the donor and the family may not be attainable under the auspices of any public charity. The objectives and the expected accomplishments may be very particular and pointed. In many public charities, even very significant gifts can quickly lose both their individuality and the identity intended by the donor.

PRIVATE FOUNDATIONS AS REMAINDERMAN BENEFICIARIES

The private foundation serves as a very important vehicle for charitable giving in the United States. Without them many donors would find it difficult if not impossible to accomplish their charitable objectives. Many affluent individuals and families have found that the private family foundation offers to them and their children the opportunity to come together as a family unit and promote charitable endeavors as a family project. This involves all the generations and serves as a very useful tool in teaching moral and social values.

Many donors feel that by creating a private family foundation they have passed onto their heirs one of the greatest gifts possible: the gift of involving the next generation in making economic and charitable decisions about the dispensing of family money from the foundation for the benefit of the community or a particular cause. A number of donors can attest to the growth experience this has provided for their children.

Other reasons for establishing a private foundation range from the personal control aspects such as annually deciding what organizations receive the foundation funds and satisfaction to the need for peer or community recognition. Quite often there is not one particular reason for creating a private foundation but a combination of a few. Control is a major impetus for establishment. There may be a particular issue or cause that a donor feels is not being addressed or explored and will not be unless the donor creates a vehicle. The issue can be personal, such as finding a cure for a disease that a member of the donor's family has contracted or funding a museum to house a personal art collection.

The financial grants made by the family foundation could also revolve around something that needs to be done for the local community, such as providing funding for a local self-help effort or founding a local community theater. The ongoing involvement of the donor and the family in a community endeavor may be what is needed to give some of the family members the prestige they require to feel that they are more meaningful community citizens. The reasons for the establishment of a private foundation can be varied and the results can be extraordinary.

Private foundations are not that easy to define. They are described in the tax code by exception rather than by an exact definition. In essence, this creates the situation where all charitable organizations are viewed as private foundations unless they are qualified under one of the exceptions to the private foundation rules.[11] The easiest way to determine whether a charity is a private foundation is to view the underlying support of the organization. Every public charity will have broad based support by the general public. The private foundation will not.

TYPES OF PRIVATE FOUNDATIONS

There are three basic types of private foundations: operating, pass-through, and pooled-fund.[12] An operating foundation is one that will each year directly dispense all income in pursuit of the objectives for which the private foundation was formed. A pass-through foundation is also referred to as a nonoperating foundation. Each year within two and one-half months after the close of the year. The pass-through foundation will make dispersals out of the principal of the foundation equal to the contribution from the preceding year.

A charitable remainder trust can have as a remainder beneficiary either an operating or nonoperating private foundation.[13] The charitable trust document should restrict the type of private foundations that can be named as a remainder interest beneficiary in charitable trust. Without this clause, the determination of the correct income tax deduction will not be possible.

Gifts of appreciated assets to private operating foundations are normally deductible at current market value. This is not true of appreciated asset gifts to nonoperating foundations. These are deductible for income tax purposes at cost rather than fair market value. Publicly traded stock was exempted from this cost-basis deduction. This exemption has expired and been revived by Congress a number of times. It last expired at the end of 1994.[14] Checking current regulations will be required in order to determine the actual basis for income tax deduction purposes if a nonoperating foundation is either used or contemplated as the remainder beneficiary.

The pooled fund is also a nonoperating private foundation organized around one or more public charities.[15] These funds pool all the contributions from the various donors, and within two and one-half months after the end of the year, disperse the income from the foundation. The donors retain the right to designate the charities that receive the income. At the death of the donor or the donor's spouse, the assets of the foundation must be distributed to the named public charities.

TAX CONSIDERATIONS FOR PRIVATE FOUNDATIONS

Contributions to a private foundation will also be subject to a different level of income tax deductibility than will those to a public charity. This is a more restrictive than liberal limit.[16] There are also a number of tax rules and regulations regarding the operation of private foundations. As there is a much greater involvement by the donor in the operational phase of a private foundation, the tax qualification rules for the purposes of income, gift, or estate tax deductibility will be more stringent.

From an income tax standpoint, a contribution to a private foundation does not qualify for a 50 percent income tax deduction. The maximum deduction s allowed is 30 percent of adjusted gross income.[17] If the property donated to the charitable trust is appreciated property, the deduction is limited to 20 percent.[18] Other than for the contribution of appreciated stock, a further reduction of the value of the gift by the amount of capital gains is included in the fair market valuation. The exception for appreciated stock is renewed periodically. Verifying that it is currently in force before relying on it is essential.

A significant number of rules and regulations are designed to prevent abuses of a private foundation by the individual creating it. One such abuse is self-dealing between the foundation and donor and other "disqualified persons," or "substantial contributor." The disqualified persons and substantial contributor group includes such parties as the members of the donor's family, the foundation manager, a government official, and any corporation, partnership, trust or unincorporated business where the donor is more than a 20 percent owner. There are also a number of restricted investment procedures.

Self-dealing is the one issue that will present the most practical problems to certain donors. The basic rule of thumb for the donor is to deal with the private foundation at arm's length. If the donor does not deal with the private foundation in this way, the donor may be subjecting himself or herself to excise tax penalties. Most of the self-dealing rules have resulted from situations over the years between donors and their private foundations that have resulted in abuses of the system. A donor is responsible for being aware of all the rules and strictly adhering to them. Any financial transaction between the donor and the private foundation should be carefully checked by competent advisors before being enacted. The penalties for self-dealing can be serious.[19]

In addition to the self-dealing regulations, there are a number of other so-called prohibited transactions that if entered into by a private foundation will result in severe penalties being assessed. These involve such areas as failing to distribute the minimum amount of income required for its tax-exempt status.[20] Paying for lobbying or other political activities in an attempt to influence the outcome of elections or a piece of legislation is also a prohibited activity for a private foundation.[21] Investments that violate the percentage rules or that put the tax-exempt purpose of the private foundation in jeopardy are also prohibited.[22]

In spite of the numerous rules and regulations affecting private foundations, more and more are being established each year. Most of the rules and regulations are there to safeguard the assets for their intended tax-exempt purpose. They are not as onerous as they appear; in fact, they are quite manageable. There are also a number of competent organizations that are designed to assist the potential donor in establishing a private foundation and in its annual administration.

One of the more recent developments is organizations that will provide the grant-making assistance that many private foundations are incapable of creating without very large expenditures. These organizations will research various grant-making possibilities, provide the written proposal, and shepherd the process to completion. They have proved invaluable to the smaller, private foundation.

One of the important considerations in viewing the establishment of a private foundation is the size of the contribution that will create it and the ultimate intended size of the principal. The funding of a private foundation should become rather substantial. If this does not occur, the operational and administrative charges may become very significant in relation to the income and principal.

COMMUNITY FOUNDATION AS REMAINDERMAN BENEFICIARIES

For those donors who find the rules and regulations of a private foundation too difficult and costly to follow, there is another alternative. In recent years in communities all over the country, a number of community foundations have come into existence. There are now over four hundred community foundations in the country. There also at least one or two national community foundations. These organizations operate in a similar mode to the local community foundation but have a national scope.[23]

The local community foundations range in size from smaller ones with assets under five million dollars to larger ones with assets in the hundreds of millions of dollars. The New York Community Foundation, the largest in the country, has assets over one billion dollars.[24] The grant-making capabilities of these community foundations can have an enormous impact upon the members of that community. The larger community foundations are now making annual grants into the tens of millions of dollars. By their very nature, these grants benefit organizations in the local community that follow the exempt purpose of the individual funds within the community foundation. The impact on the local communities of these grant-making capacities is enormous and growing significantly.

Community foundations serve as a bridge between private foundations and public charities. A community foundation is a public charity the same as all other public charities. It raises money, but in a different manner. The fund-raising activities of a community foundation consist of attracting from the community individual funds in the form of private foundations. These individual funds are collected under the auspices of the community foundation and operated by its board. The majority of the individual funds that comprise most community foundations were received by the foundation as bequests. These individual funds comprise either those private foundations that were in existence while the donor was alive or ones created at the death of the donor. The other major source of individual funds are those private foundations that for a variety of reasons are collapsed and brought under the auspices of the community foundation.

Contributions to a community foundation are eligible for the same maximum 50 percent deduction available to all other public charities.[25] In addition to the increased deduction possibilities, by utilizing the community foundation as the beneficiary the donor can forgo the majority of the cost of operating her or his own private foundation. The donor does not, however, have to forgo the benefits. The family can still be involved in grant-making activities. The final OK belongs to the board of the community foundation, but they will be cognizant of the advice and consultation of the family of the donor in reaching these decisions. The identity of the individual fund is maintained by the community foundation. The grant making done is from that fund and recognized as such. The grant making follows the exempt purpose of the fund in all of its activities.

There are basically three broad categories of gifts to community foundations. The first type is the unrestricted gift. In this case, a fund is established under the auspices of the community foundation. The board of the community foundation decides the grant making for this gift—what organizations will be funded by the individual fund. There are no restrictions put on these decisions. The second type is the advised fund, which is a segregated account; family nominators are designated to assist in the grant making. The community foundation will normally recognize this advisory relationship for two subsequent generations after the donor's. The third type is the supporting organization, which consists of a joint board with the family appointing a minority member.

In many situations, naming an individual foundation under the auspices of a community foundation as the remainder interest in a charitable remainder trust is a very practical decision for a donor. The donor is able to acquire the majority of the benefits resulting from a private foundation being the remainderman yet knows that the assets will not be subject to enormous administrative cost and fees. The donor also has the comfort of knowing that there will be competent management responsible not only for the management of the assets but also for the grant-making responsibilities.

Chapter Twelve

Case Histories

In order to create a more in-depth understanding of the effectiveness of the charitable remainder trust, this chapter will explore four cases that illustrate its flexibility.

THE EXECUTIVE

The first situation we are going to examine involves Henry and Kathy Lineberg. Henry is 63 and Kathy is 56. Henry has spent the last 25 years with the same publishing company and has risen to the rank of senior vice president. The company's president for the last 15 years retired last year, and the new president has gradually replaced upper-echelon management. Henry has had inklings that he may be on that replacement list.

The executive bonus structure that has been in place for the last 10 years has been revamped, and Henry is faced with a $50,000 reduction in this year's income. Henry and Kathy have had a number of serious discussions regarding their plans in the event that he is asked to take early retirement. He really doesn't want to retire but may be offered a retirement package that would be very difficult to refuse. A few of his counterparts from other departments have already agreed to exercise this option. The retirement offer that has been extended to the other executives is one that would increase his current retirement benefit to a level equal to what he would have received at age 65.

Being a very methodical person, Henry has discussed his situation with a few of the executives who are in his same position and has been referred to a financial planner with whom a few of them have worked. The financial planner, Seymour Glending, is a specialist who works with executives such as Henry. Henry and

Kathy subsequently arrange an appointment with Seymour at his office. During their initial meeting, Seymour details his working arrangement with his clients and discusses his fee arrangement. The Linebergs agree to the arrangement and contract with Seymour for his services.

During the initial data-gathering session, Seymour learns the following information. With his current bonus reduction, Henry will earn a gross income of $325,000 this year. Kathy works part-time in a friend's boutique and earns about $25,000 a year. Henry and Kathy do not have any children and do not have any close relatives. Both their parents are dead. Henry had a brother who died during his teens, and Kathy was an only child. They own their home, which has no mortgage. It currently has a fair market value of $500,000. Henry has always considered himself a conservative investor. They have an investment portfolio of approximately $800,000, consisting of $500,000 in Treasury bonds and bills, $150,000 in corporate stock, and the balance in certificates of deposit.

The only other investment they have is stock in Henry's company, which was acquired over the initial 20 years of Henry's employment. Henry does not consider this part of his investment portfolio, as he has never sold any of the stock and has for the last 10 years regarded it as part of his retirement planning assets. In compiling the various purchases, Henry and Seymour total up the acquisition costs to only $27,340. If the stock were to be liquidated today, that would represent a capital gain of $891,660.

In addition to the investment portfolio, Henry has both a deferred compensation plan with the company and as a pension and profit-sharing plan. The deferred compensation plan is currently not funded. This will amount to $5,750 per month for Henry at retirement. It can only be received as monthly income. Henry will receive at normal retirement age a supplemental retirement benefit. Henry is fully vested in this plan. In the pension plan, Henry has a $950,000 lump sum value, approximately. The profit-sharing plan has a vested benefit of $750,000. This is all invested in company stock. In addition to these retirement assets, the Linebergs have another $53,000 in individual retirement accounts invested in money market funds.

The Lineberg's assets total $4,053,000 of which almost 50 percent of their investable assets are in one issue, Henry's company stock. This is also a very fluctuating asset. The stock is publicly traded, although very thinly. In the average week, about 10 thousand shares change hands. The price of the stock fluctuated in the last 18 months from a high of $155 to a low of $65 per share. The history of this stock follows this same pattern. The stock moves very quickly up or down, based upon the popularity of the books published by Henry's firm. The current market value is $100 per share. The market price of the shares five months ago was $137 per share. In the last 18 months, Henry and Kathy watched their wealth decline on paper by $647,000. It is now on the rebound as a number of successful novels have hit the best seller list and the stock price has gained strength. This hardly presents the picture of the conservative investor that Henry imagined himself to be.

In the data-gathering meetings, Seymour also explores their retirement objectives, income needs, and estate asset-distribution plan. As Henry and Kathy do not have any immediate family in the area, they do not feel the need to stay there after Henry retires. They have traveled quite a bit in the Southwest and have always envisioned themselves retiring there. They have not really decided where but are leaning towards Arizona. They are planning on looking for a retirement home on their next trip out West.

In reviewing their recent income tax return, Seymour notices they do not have many deductions, particulary consequential charitable deductions. The major charitable deduction is expenses entailed by Kathy in her volunteer charitable work. In questioning them about this, Seymour learns that Kathy, never having had any children of her own, has become deeply involved with an organization that provides assistance to young children afflicted with crippling diseases. She has been instrumental in raising funds for them and assisting in their programs. Of late, Kathy has gotten Henry involved in many of the social functions of this organization.

The Linebergs had lived with these ups and downs of the share price in Henry's company, always believing that the stock price would rebound. They had no intention of selling the stock during those years, so the actual share price did not have any real meaning to them. Now that Henry's retirement date is fast approaching, this price fluctuation has become an important consideration; in fact, they now follow the stock price daily and discuss their options with each other almost every evening. They have come to the conclusion that in order to be sure their retirement years are secure, they will start selling the stock and invest the proceeds of the sale in more secure investments.

In reviewing the conclusion that the Linebergs have reached, Seymour tells them that the capital gains tax on the sale, including the state tax, is going to be over $300,000. The Linebergs knew there would be a tax due but had never calculated the impact of this tax on their retirement income. The loss of monthly earnings at an 8 percent return would total over $2,000 per month. Kathy, in particular, is shocked at this outcome. She asks what alternatives are available to counter this erosion.

Seymour mentions that there is one that might serve a couple of purposes and explains the concept of social capital and charitable remainder trusts. He first spends some time reviewing the concept of social capital and self-directed philanthropy. He then brings up the children's organization with which Kathy is so involved. He poses the following question to them: "How would you like to benefit the children while at the same time benefiting yourselves?"

The answer is relatively easy for the Linebergs. Once they decide to explore the option of the charitable remainder trust, the rest of the steps necessary to solidify their financial program start to fall into place. Table 12–1 illustrates the impact of the charitable remainder trust (NIMCRUT) on their financial picture.

As Table 12–1 illustrates, the advantages to the Linebergs from the use of the charitable remainder trust are substantial. The net spendable income over both lives is increased by 86 percent. Attaining this type of increase without the use of the charitable remainder trust would require a rate of return on the remainder value at an extraordinary rate. The estate tax, on this particular asset, as it is no longer in the Lineberg's asset base, is totally eliminated. As there is nothing left in the estate from this asset, there will be nothing bequeathed to an heir. This does not present a

TABLE 12–1
NIMCRUT Comparison

Assumptions

Stock growth rate	4.5%
Stock dividend rate	2.5%
Income rate for outright sale example	8%
Rate for CRT	Two-year deferral period—2% Yield—6% Growth
	Balance of years—6% Yield—2% Growth
Income tax rate	40% (combined state and federal)
Long-term capital gains rate	36% (combined state and federal)
Estate tax rate	55%

Asset Analysis	Outright Sale	Charitable Remainder Trust
Current value of asset	$919,000	$919,000
Adjusted cost basis (−)	27,340	27,340
Capital gain on sale	891,660	891,660
Capital gains tax (36%)(−)	321,090	0
Remainder to invest	$498,570	$919,000
Income Analysis		
Annual gross income (8%)	$39,885	$73,520
Annual net income (after 40% tax)	23,931	44,112
Life expectancy (years)	28	28
Lifetime net income (total)	670,068	1,235,136
Charitable income tax deduction	0	138,021
Personal income tax rate	40	40
Deduction tax savings	0	55,208
Lifetime spendable income	$670,068	$1,290,344
Estate Analysis		
Value in estate	$498,570	$0
Estate tax (55%)(−)	274,213	0
Net to heirs	$224,357	$0
Benefit Summary		
Spendable income	$670,068	$1,290,344
Estate to heirs	224,357	0
Total	$894,425	$1,290,344
Philanthropic contributions		
Involuntary	224,357	0
Voluntary	0	1,000,000
Total benefits	$894,425	$2,290,344

Source: American Renaissance Trust Information Services. Version 3.01 © 1992 PhilanthroTec, Inc.

problem for the Linebergs, as they are not interested in leaving assets to heirs.

The social capital applications of the dollars diverted from capital gains and estate taxes are an additional motivation for the Linebergs. They are more interested in seeing their tax dollars diverted to Kathy's special interest in the children's charity than having them become part of the tax revenue stream. Kathy also feels that whether they stay here or move out West the increased annual income stream will be useful, not only for lifestyle support, but also for any annual needs that might develop with her charitable interest.

Another important feature of this plan is the diversity that is attained in the Lineberg's investment portfolio. Once the stock has been transferred into the trust, Seymour and Henry, along with the money manager, devise a strategy to gradually dispose of the stock at a certain price level. Henry feels that all the changes occurring within the company will have a favorable impact on the share price. The other factor affecting the sale of the securities is the small turnover of shares each week. In order to be assured of not disrupting the market, they arrange for a timed disposition of the stock. Initially, Henry agrees to sell $50,000 worth of shares when the purchase price per share exceeds $110.

Henry drafts a letter to that effect, adding that additional sales of $50,000 lots can be made at a price level of $120, and as much stock as possible can be sold if the stock reaches $130 per share. The letter further states that if at the end of a six-month period, the price of the shares has not risen to $120, the sale strategy will be reviewed. Since current income is not a major need for the Linebergs and they have adopted a net income with makeup charitable remainder unitrust, this plan is very workable.

The added financial incentives that the Linebergs received via means of the charitable gift are another important consideration for them. The income tax deduction resulting from the gift amounts to $138,021, for a tax savings of $55,208. The avoidance of the capital gain tax on sale of the stock results in a tax savings of $321,091. The total actual tax savings for the Lineberg's in their income tax bracket is $376,299. This tax savings is the catalyst to fueling the dramatic increase in net spendable income developed by the charitable remainder trust.

When all of the positive factors regarding the charitable remainder trust are considered, they more than outweigh the single negative result: loss of control of the principal. Many older prospective donors find this concern a difficult hurdle to overcome. Quite often, no matter the amount of the assets, there is either a disclosed or undisclosed fear of running out of money in one's later years. Transferring an asset into an irrevocable trust can develop into a traumatic decision for some people. Fortunately, the Linebergs have a very good understanding of the control factor and are not concerned with it. Those donors who do not understand need to have emphasized to them the guarantee features of the income stream of the typical charitable remainder trust.

THE BUSINESS OWNER

Stanley and Olivia Mather own and currently operate a very profitable warehousing business. Stanley is 64 and Olivia is 62. Their business value, including the warehouse properties, is approximately $6,000,000. The rest of their assets, including their home, investments, and personal property, amount to another $1,000,000. They have two children, both of whom are married, have children, and have their own careers. Neither of the children are ever going to come into the warehouse business. For the past two years, the Mathers have been contemplating selling their business and retiring. In fact, they have been approached by a major national warehouse chain on a possible purchase.

The business is likely to realize the full $6,000,000 on sale. Recently, Stanley went to his doctor for a physical and was given quite a scare. His EKG showed some variations in readings from previous ones, and he was referred to a cardiologist who put him through some intensive testing. Everything came out all right, and he was given a clean bill of health. His doctor did suggest that he slow down a little, however, as his blood pressure was slightly elevated.

Stanley, being somewhat of a hypochondriac, is very concerned about this development and after a discussion with Olivia decides to formally look for a buyer for their business. Stanley consults with their accountant on the tax ramifications of this transaction. As the Mathers have virtually no cost basis in the company stock, he informs them that the taxes on the sale would amount to more than $1,600,000. Needless to say, this is not a happy revelation. As the Mathers have not had a comprehensive financial plan done for them and the need is now evident, the accountant refers them to a specialist in his office. After a series of meetings, the financial planning specialist develops a few major themes, to which the Mathers agree.

The primary consideration is the development of a retirement program that will provide them with the ability to maintain their current standard of living. They are currently netting approximately $300,000 annually from the business and feel comfortable in replicating this. They want to avoid, as much as possible, the dissolution of the sale price of their business due to taxes. Their youngest grandchild was born with a physical deformity and has already had extensive therapy at a regional children's hospital and will require additional years of therapy. They feel a strong obligation to this hospital, as it extended a significant amount of reduced fee services to their daughter for their grandchild. They want to do something in the future to repay the hospital for the kindness extended to their family. Their final interest is in passing as much of their estate as possible to their children.

The financial advisor does the preliminary financial and estate calculations, combining all of this information into a social capital program built around the assembly of the necessary team of expert advisors to effect the desired plan. The Mathers wholeheartedly agree. After several consultations, the professional advisory team develops a basic scenario. The Mathers, in the meantime, contact the corporation that had previously approached them regarding the acquisition of their company. They are still very interested in the purchase of the entire operation. Stanley conveys this information to the financial advisor. This data helps to solidify the final plan recommendations.

As the Mathers wish to have sufficient funds for their retirement, the advisory team recommends they transfer only 75 percent of their company stock into a charitable remainder trust, with the remainder beneficiary being the hospital. Both the Mathers and the trust will sell their stock to the same buyer. There will be an income tax deduction available for the transfer into the charitable trust of the bulk of the stock. This deduction will be over $900,000 and will offset almost two-thirds of the capital gains produced on the sale of the stock on a personal basis.

In order to guarantee that their children receive their rightful inheritance, they also establish a wealth replacement trust to benefit them and their families, funded with a $4,500,000 life insurance policy, paid for with part of the income received from the charitable trust. The premiums for the insurance will be gifted into the wealth replacement trust under the annual gift tax exclusion allowance. They also plan, at their deaths, to leave the maximum unified credit of $600,000 to the children, leaving very little of the estate subject to estate taxes. The comparison of a plan involving the outright sale of the company and the social capital solution is detailed in Table 12–2.

As Table 12–2 illustrates, the overall benefits to the Mathers and their children are substantial. They are able to effect the sale of their business on a tax-favorable basis. Instead of paying a sizable capital gains tax, they are able to virtually eliminate the tax via means of the combination of the charitable gift and personal sale. If this total deduction cannot be fully realized in the first year, whatever portion that is not used can be carried forward and deducted in a future year. The resultant income generated is 35 percent higher under the charitable gift scenario than under the illustration of the stock sale.

In electing to replace the entire value of the donated property to their children, the Mathers assumed an ongoing life insurance premium of $60,000. This premium will be paid over a period of 15 years. After the premium payment period, the net spendable income payable to them will be increased by that amount. Had they elected to give their children the net value after estate taxes of their business asset as if they had retained it until their death, the insurance approach would be different. The face amount of the life insurance purchased would be for approximately one-half of this amount. The ensuing annual premium would be proportionately reduced, thereby freeing up more spendable income. The selection of the face amount of the life insurance in the wealth replacement trust, left for the benefit of the heirs, is a variable decision based upon the desires of the donors.

TABLE 12–2
Mather Comparison

Assumptions

Trust payout rate	8%	Capital gains tax	28%
Trust investment rate of return	8%	Estate tax rate	50%
Income tax rate	31%		

Asset Analysis	Outright Sale	Charitable Remainder Trust
Value of stock	$6,000,000	$6,000,000
Gift to trust	0	4,500,000
Capital gains portion	6,000,000	1,500,000
Charitable deduction (−)	0	927,765
Taxable gain (=)	6,000,000	572,235
Tax due on sale (28%)(−)	1,680,000	160,225
Capital left to invest	4,320,000	5,839,775
Annual taxable income (8%)	345,600	467,182
Net after tax income (31%)	238,464	322,356
Life insurance premium (−)	0	60,000
Net spendable income (=)	238,464	262,356
Net spendable income over life expectancies	$5,961,600	$7,156,075
Estate Analysis		
After tax proceeds of sale	$4,320,000	$1,339,775
Other assets (+)	1,000,000	1,000,000
Total personal assets (=)	5,320,000	2,339,775
Assets-charitable trust (+)	0	4,500,000
Gross estate (=)	5,320,000	6,839,775
Charitable deduction (−)	0	4,500,000
Taxable estate (=)	5,320,000	2,339,775
Estate tax due (−)	2,266,000	455,910
Net estate to heirs (=)	3,054,400	1,883,865
Life insurance benefit (+)	0	4,500,000
Heirs benefit (=)	3,054,400	6,383,865
Mather Hospital Foundation	$0	$4,500,000
Summary of Social Capital		
Capital gain and estate taxes (involuntary philanthropy)	$3,946,000	$616,135
Charitable gift (voluntary philanthropy)	$0	$4,500,000
Summary of Financial Capital		
Income	$5,961,600	$7,156,075
Heirs' inheritance (+)	3,054,400	6,383,865
Total personal financial capital (=)	$9,016,000	$13,539,940

Source: American Renaissance Trust Information Services. Version 3.01 © 1992
PhilanthroTec, Inc.

By electing the social capital approach to the distribution of their assets, the Mathers were able to maximize their income during retirement from the sale of the business. This is accomplished at the same time they are creating a larger inheritance for their children, through the use of the wealth replacement trust, in conjunction with the other estate-planning techniques. They also dramatically reduced the involuntary philanthropy of estate taxes occurring at their death and turned the Mather Hospital Foundation into a family mission that the children and grandchildren will now be able to continue. The children and grandchildren will now be responsible each year for the dispersal of funds from the family foundation for the benefit of the hospital. This therefore becomes a major portion of the Mathers living legacy.

THE WIDOWER

Jason Edwards is a 74-year-old widower. He and his wife Amy were married for 40 years. She died five years ago from cancer. Their child died at age two, and they never had another. Jason has been retired from his position as a bank manager since age 65. He lives on a modest pension and his monthly social security. His total monthly income is approximately $3,000. Other than a few cousins, Jason has no other close relatives.

Jason spends quite a bit of his time at the senior citizen center sponsored by the local church. He attends most of the trips and seminars sponsored by the center. At a session regarding elder-care and legal and financial planning, he is intrigued with a number of the examples of asset protection discussed by the attorney giving the seminar. One in particular that piques his interest is the story of a widow who was living on a modest income who donated a valuable painting to her church and received back from the church an annual income for life. He does not have a valuable painting, but he does have something that he thinks might be of considerable worth.

Back in the early 20s, his wife's father had started his career as a musical songwriter. He had died in his early 70s, and one of the items Jason's wife had received was a trunk filled with original scores of a large number of songs on which her father had collaborated. She and Jason didn't think they were worth a lot of money, but she had kept them as a remembrance of her father. They are still in the trunk in Jason's attic. He recently read an article about how valuable certain older original musical scores had become. He approaches the lawyer presenting the seminar and is further encouraged by his reaction. The attorney professes not to be an expert in these types of assets but does arrange a meeting with Jason and the member of the firm who specializes in those matters.

After doing some investigation, they are able to determine that indeed there may be some value to the song sheets. It seems that a thriving collectors market has developed in that area. In order to get an appraisal, Jason ships a few of the song sheets to an auction firm that specializes in that type of memorabilia. The initial appraisal comes back at anywhere between $4,000 to $5,000 per song. Jason knows there are over 100 individual song sheets. With the attorney, he develops a strategy to convert those song sheets into an income stream. They view a scenario that compares both a sale and a gift to Jason's church. The charitable gift is structured as a charitable remainder trust. The resultant calculation comparisons are illustrated in Table 12–3.

Jason and his wife had always thought about being able to do something of consequence with their assets for the benefit of their church. Jason had not, however, changed his will since his wife's death to reflect this desire. Other than distant cousins, there are not any relatives to whom the assets should pass. After reviewing the above figures and calculating the value of the rest of his assets, he decides to leave the remainder of his estate, other than a few modest bequests to named individuals, to the church and the local conservation society.

Jason is extremely pleased by the projected 38 percent increase in spendable income. In order to realize this income stream, the music scores must first be liquidated. After consultation with the attorney and his financial advisor, he agrees to create a standard charitable remainder unitrust. He will gift the music scores into this trust and appoint a special independent trustee to obtain an appraisal of the gift and arrange for the sale. The attorney

TABLE 12–3
Edwards Comparison

Assumptions		
Trust payout rate	8%	
Investment rate of return	8%	
Income tax rate	31%	
Capital gains tax	28%	
Estate tax rate	40%	

Asset Analysis	Outright Sale	Charitable Remainder Trust
Asset value	$500,000	$500,000
Capital gain realized	500,000	0
Capital gain tax (28%)(−)	140,000	0
Net amount to invest (=)	$360,000	$500,000
Income and Cash Flow Analysis		
Annual gross income (8%)	$28,800	$40,000
After-tax income (31%)	19,872	27,600
Life expectancy (x)	11	11
Lifetime net income (=)	218,592	303,600
Charitable income tax deduction	$0	$0
Estate Analysis		
Asset estate value	$360,000	$0
Estate tax	144,000	0
Net to heirs	$216,000	$0
Summary of Social Capital		
Total capital gain and estate tax (involuntary philanthropy)	$284,000	$0
Charitable gift (voluntary philanthropy)	$0	$500,000
Summary of Personal Capital		
Income	$218,592	$303,600
Benefits to heirs (+)	216,000	0
Total personal capital (=)	$434,592	$303,600
Total Capital		
Income	$218,592	$303,600
Bequests	216,000	500,000
Total	$434,592	$803,600

Source: American Renaissance Trust Information Services. Version 3.01 © 1992 PhilanthroTec, Inc.

drafts the necessary trust documents to accomplish this, and Jason creates the trust. The detailed appraisal and subsequent sale results in a net of $500,000 after all expenses. This will comprise the trust principal.

In the above figures, there is no notation of a charitable income tax deduction for the gift of the song sheets into the charitable remainder trust. Normally, when a donation is made into a charitable remainder trust, an income tax deduction is created for the value of the remainder interest left to the charitable organization. When the property donated to a charitable remainder trust consists of appreciated tangible personal property, it is extremely difficult to develop an income tax deduction for the market value.

In order to obtain an income tax deduction for the current market value of appreciated tangible personal property the income tax deduction rules, as previously discussed in Chapter Eight, require that these type of gifts be made to like institutions. Even in the case of a painting given to a museum, if a charitable remainder trust is the conduit, the gift must be sold to produce funds that can be allocated into income-producing investments. In such circumstances, the exemption for a market-value deduction is not available. The deduction basis will become the acquisition cost of the property. Since Jason has no means of determining the basis of the property, at the time of his father-in-law's death, the ability to take a deduction is not available. If he could establish a cost basis, a modest income tax deduction might be developed.

Adopting a social capital approach to the disposition of his assets has added a new dimension to Jason's life. More than ever, he feels a strong kinship with the other members of his senior citizen group and his church. They have become his family, and the ability to take positive action—to assure their continuance through his charitable gifts—is a strong motivation for him. He becomes a strong proponent of the social capital approach to the disposition of one's assets and is encouraged by the minister to speak at various other senior citizen centers regarding his actions. This development adds a new dimension to his retirement years and one that he comes to treasure.

THE CORPORATION

An innovative use of a charitable remainder trust is to reposition a corporate asset both to obtain favorable tax treatment on its disposal and to provide an income stream to either the stockholders or a selected party. This is accomplished while providing the ability to gift the remainder interest to a charitable entity. The four Simpson brothers equally own a television production company. They have been in business for over 20 years and operate as a subchapter S corporation. In addition to producing new television shows, over the years they have built a significant library of original old films. One part of this collection is the entire work of an early Hollywood comedian. They have recently been approached by a private collector who asked if they were willing to part with these films.

They reviewed their records and were able to ascertain that the cost basis of the films was $200,000. Before proceeding any further, they contact their accountant to discuss the best way of handling the sale from an income tax point of view. He advises them that, as they are a subchapter S corporation, all capital gains from the sale would flow directly out to each of them and be taxed on a personal basis at the current capital gains tax rate of 28 percent. He also reviews other methods of structuring the disposal of the property, such as an installment sale. Each of the ways he explores results in an increase in personal income taxes. They ask what alternatives there are to this tax scenario and are advised that there aren't any, other than giving the asset away to a charitable organization before the sale is consummated.

The brothers ask to have the ways of accomplishing this explored and are advised of the following alternatives. One way is an outright gift to a charity. In this case, they would receive as a personal benefit through the subchapter S an income tax deduction for the full market value of the films equal to their pro-rata share of the subchapter S stock. The other charitable gift method is the use of a charitable remainder trust. In this case, they would receive only a partial income tax deduction. In return for a loss of a portion of the deduction, they would receive an income stream from the charitable remainder trust for a period of 20 years. As the asset is owned by a corporate entity, the maximum period for receipt of income would be 20 years.[1]

The four brothers discuss the matter and agree that the approach makes a great deal of sense. Each of them, through their wives, has been passively involved with charitable organizations for a number of years. Donating to charities is a very common occurrence in their lives, so the concept of utilizing a charitable trust to accomplish the sale of the films is easily assimilated. In order to have some idea of the value of the films, they have them appraised. The appraisal value is a substantial increase over their purchase price. They decide to gift the films into a charitable remainder trust that is created by the corporation. Each of them, as an equal subchapter S stockholder, will receive an equal income distribution from the trust.

After the films have been gifted into the trust but before the actual sale, the trustee must obtain an appraisal of the property. In order to assure that this appraisal is completely independent of all parties concerned, a special independent trustee is interjected into the process. The role of the special independent trustee is to obtain a new qualified appraisal and arrange for the sale of the films. The appraisal of $1,000,000 done for the special independent trustee is almost identical to the one the Simpson brothers previously obtained. The potential buyer is now contacted, and sale negotiations are started. A price is finally agreed upon, at a little over the appraisal value. Once all the expenses of the sale have been deducted, the net to the charitable remainder trust is $1,000,000. Table 12–4 illustrates the results of this transaction for a representative individual brother.

Needless to say, the Simpson brothers are delighted by the results of this transaction. Their wives, who are the ones who are very actively involved with the charitable organizations, are equally delighted by the prospects of eventually creating an endowment for their favorite charity. The charities, in turn, hope to utilize them as role models for other donors with appreciated assets, to encourage like kinds of gifts. In addition to the gains on the charitable side, the Simpsons realize a substantial increase in the income stream flowing from the sale of the films.

By repositioning this corporate asset into the charitable remainder trust, the Simpsons are able to execute the sale and realize a 20 percent increase in income. This increase in income, on

TABLE 12–4
Simpson Comparison

Assumptions

Trust payout rate	8%
Investment rate of return	8%
Income tax rate	31%
Capital gains rate	28%
Estate tax rate	50%

Asset Analysis	Outright Sale	Charitable Remainder Trust
Current value of asset	$250,000	$250,000
Adjusted cost basis (−)	50,000	50,000
Realized capital gain (=)	200,000	200,000
Capital gain tax (28%)	56,000	0
Net funds to invest (=)	$194,000	$250,000

Income Analysis

Annual gross income (8%)	$15,520	$20,000
Annual net income (31% tax)	10,709	13,800
Term certain (x)	20	20
Lifetime net income (=)	214,180	276,000
Total lifetime net income	$214,180	$300,366

Estate Analysis

Estate asset value	$194,000	$0
Estate tax	97,000	0
Net to heirs (=)	$97,000	$0

Summary of Social Capital

Capital gain and estate tax (involuntary philanthropy)	$153,000	$0
Charitable gift (voluntary philanthropy)	$0	250,000

Summary of Personal Capital

Lifetime income	$214,180	$300,366
Net to heirs	97,000	0
Total personal capital	$311,080	$300,366

Total Capital

Lifetime income	$214,180	$300,366
Bequests	97,000	250,000
Total	$311,080	$550,366

Source: American Renaissance Trust Information Services. Version 3.01 © 1992 PhilanthroTec, Inc.

a present-value interest basis, would more than offset the loss of the remaining principal at the end of the 20-year income period. In addition, if the underlying asset yielded a better return than anticipated, the tax exempt environment of the charitable remainder trust would greatly enhance the accumulation. This in turn would proportionately increase the income payments to each brother.

Additionally, through the gift to their designated charity at the completion of twenty years, the brothers will be able to satisfy an obligation to which their family is strongly committed. The end result of their accountant's initial suggestion ends up bringing added benefits to them, not only in the form of increased annual income, but also in increased personal satisfaction.

Chapter Thirteen

The Present and the Future

The role of philanthropy in the 21st century will be one of increased responsibilities and increased demands. In many areas of the country and the charitable community, the demands imposed will stretch the available resources. In recent years, the number of new charitable organizations registering with the Internal Revenue Service has grown at a dramatic rate. All across this country, the need for people to help other people has never been more apparent. One only has to pick up the daily newspaper or view a local television news broadcast to be instantly reminded of the many problems and issues that face the United States.

In addition to the challenges of fund-raising, the philanthropic community must deal with a growing sense of apathy and helplessness in many communities. A segment of the general population now believes there are too many problems and that little or nothing can be done to address them. This feeling of helplessness and frustration has led many to conclude that the best course of action is to ignore the problems, and in turn they will go away. Unfortunately, the type of problems facing the country do not go away. They only increase in importance and magnitude.

One of the major challenges that the United States will face in the coming years is the rekindling of our founders' charitable spirit. This is not necessarily an issue of money, but of involvement.

President John F. Kennedy said in the 1960s, "One man can make a difference, and every man should try." That challenge of more than 30 years ago is as relevant today as it was then. Without individuals becoming more involved in assisting others, the promise of the future will be lost on a great percentage of the population.

One way to start in the financial area of their lives is for taxpayers to demand that their tax dollars be properly utilized. They can also redirect as much of their social capital as possible to charitable organizations that exemplify their ideals and goals. With the implementation of a charitable remainder trust, one man, one woman, or one couple can start to make a difference.

In trying to interpret the changes in our society that are beginning to unfold, one can reflect back upon the major ongoing trends that were identified in the first chapter. The first was the estimate of the 8 to 10 trillion dollars of assets that are currently owned and controlled by individuals in this country over age 50. The aging of the population is another ongoing trend that, combined with the dramatic growth of the percentages of minority representation in the overall census figures, has and will continue to have a dramatic impact on the country.

The size of the current federal deficit presents an imposing problem when the question of funding any new type of program arises. This problem will become much more acute as the impending impact of the aging Baby Boom generation accelerates the problem. Under current projections, the growth in the entitlement programs, for purely demographic reasons, will consume the entire federal budget sometime within the first 30 years of the next century.

The above mentioned trends will be played out over the ensuing years. The results are just starting to be interpreted and understood. Whatever the exact results, the role of government and the individual citizen will experience some dramatic shifts.

The federal government must make adequate provisions to guarantee that private funding of nonprofit activities will be allowed to continue on a tax-deductible basis. Without these provisions, the nonprofit sector will bear the risk of a major loss of funding just as the enormity of their responsibilities is increasing. In fact, the government will need to expand the financial and tax incentives for individuals and businesses in order to guarantee the required flow of monies needed to fund the increased activities of the nonprofit sector.

Since the end of World War II, American society has become increasingly mobile. As the information and knowledge age unfolds, this mobility will continue to increase at a dramatic rate. Many people have lost the sense of belonging to a community, a town, a city, or even a state. They most likely don't live where they were raised or even where they spent their early adulthood. They also may no longer work in a structured organization but may be part of a growing movement that, by the turn of the century, will mean between 30 to 50 percent of the employees of most companies will be working at home and telecommuting to the office.

The strain that this type of mobility and lack of centralized organizational location will put on the community and upon the fund-raising of many large and small charities is yet to be measured. How does an organization such as the United Way do their fund-raising and effectively reach all the employees of the company when they do not work in a central location or locations, and may not live in the same community or even state? Even if they can reach them, how do they appeal for contributions to address local concerns when these employees do not identify with the same issues as would a local office or factory worker? How does the local food bank run a food collection for the needy at an office when 50 percent of the workforce is seldom or never there? There are many questions, and the solutions will require imagination and innovation.

The typical potential donors will be more informed and more interested in reviewing and assessing the results of their actions. Their behavior and actions will follow their contributions. Their contributions in turn will follow their effective behavior and actions. They will not blindly turn over their contributions to an organization without a tremendous amount of accountability. Their access to information on the financial and social performance of the charitable organization will become automatic via means of the computer terminal.

Exceedingly efficient results will be, if they are not currently, tantamount to successful fundraising. Otherwise, the dollars will quickly go elsewhere. The individual will be in control, unlike any other time in the history of fund-raising. Reaching and keeping the donor will become a larger and more significant challenge for the charitable organization. Promoting an understanding of social capital among their donor base will become vital to the charity's economic well-being.

The individual donor in developing a thorough understanding of the concept of social capital begins to acquire the knowledge and tools to effect social change. Once implemented, the strategy of social capital can have a dramatic impact upon the lives of the individual donors involved. Once social awareness reaches the implementation stage, a number of lifestyle changes can and will take place. The individual may become much more personally involved with the charity or cause. They may even become a strong advocate or spokesperson for the organization or cause. Another lifestyle change will be in how they invest their money, both their personal funds and those designated for charitable purposes.

Once an individual fully grasps the concept of social capital, integrating it into his or her daily life becomes a relatively easy transition. Change can be effected many ways. One way to create positive change in society is for an individual to direct his or her current investment dollars into companies and organizations that promote the same ideals and beliefs that he or she does. Although there are other ways to promote the ideals of a particular charitable cause or organization in addition to direct contributions, using socially responsible investing has a tremendous multiplying effect, well in excess of the actual dollar investment.

SOCIALLY RESPONSIBLE INVESTING

The "Social Capital" activists will direct their current investable dollars into organizations that promote their social agenda. The impact of this redirection of assets can be astounding. In a book on the subject of socially responsible investing, authors Peter Kinder, Steven Lydenberg, and Amy Domini have detailed this strategy for achieving social change.[1]

Traditionally, socially responsible investing has taken one of two paths of portfolio arrangement. These procedures are directly opposed to each other. The first approach involves directing investments to companies that promote the same social agenda as the investor. The second approach is to deliberately avoid investing in companies that support a social agenda that is different from the investor's. Each of these approaches is relatively self-explanatory. In analyzing some investment decisions, the implementation of either technique is quite simple. In others, the decision-making process can become quite complex.

There is one other method of socially responsible investing that can often promote change in a corporation's activities. This is the approach of the activist shareholder. Under this methodology, an individual or organizational shareholder invests in a small amount of stock in a company in order to promote their social agenda at company shareholder meetings. Often, this approach can have a meaningful impact on a corporation's policies. Many investors are aware of this "gadfly" approach. At times, it has worked quite effectively; at other times, it has been ineffective. This investment philosophy, although useful in a number of areas, is not one that will promote the type of investment results or social change that the social capital investor wishes to achieve.

A different area of socially responsible investing, away from the larger public companies, involves organizations and projects on a much smaller level in the local community. This has become a very popular mode of socially conscious investing over recent years. The investment opportunities afforded in the local community cover a whole gamut of areas. These can range from local economic issues to ones involving very sensitive environmental concerns.

An example of a local economic issue is investments in companies or agencies that provide employment in the local community. The investments could range from providing seed capital to start-up organizations to investments in bonds in local business enterprise zones.

A local environmental investment could provide the funding for the purchase of land for conservation purposes or to help purchase a house that should be preserved for its historical and cultural value.

The most common misconception about socially responsible investors is that they must be willing to sacrifice growth and yield in order to further their social agenda. There is a sufficient amount of historical evidence available from a variety of sources that completely discounts this notion. The socially responsible investor will, on average, receive a rate of return equivalent to market returns in the same type of investments. Some years, it will be higher; some years, it will be lower. But the overall return should not vary that much from similar, nonsocially responsive investments.

There are basically three ways that an investor can create a socially responsible portfolio. The first two ways are by accessing groups of professionals that offer socially responsible investors access to the investment market. These professionals are either mutual fund companies or money managers. The third method for the individual to invest is through direct personal selection of particular companies. The majority of the time, the personal selection investment route will prove a more time-consuming and daunting experience than will the approach of utilizing professional advisors.

The professionals provide a great degree of research to the investor in regard to their particular social agenda and how that interfaces with an investment in a particular company. This research can be provided by the mutual fund company or by the individual money manager. It may also be purchased by the professional advisor from a commercial source. A variety of organizations provide services to assist the professional manager in ascertaining certain information about a particular company.

This research is provided primarily in the form of social screens. There are two major screening techniques. One involves screening away companies that operate in ways that are in deference to the social agenda of the investor. The other method involves screening companies whose operating philosophy or products support the social agenda of the investor. These are both relatively self-explanatory. Screening away is an avoidance mechanism that denotes investments in companies and industries that promote products or agendas that are contrary to the social objectives of that type of investor. These will range from such obvious areas as tobacco-related products or nuclear energy to a number of not so easily detected areas such as human rights and work rules.

Screening toward investments that promote a significant social agenda or program is the other general screening technique.

This could involve finding companies that have a "green agenda," such as promoting recycling and other environmental issues. These could be obvious and easily detected or very subtle, requiring a greater degree of investigation and scrutiny.

Whether screening away or screening for a particular area, the effectiveness of the entire process involves a number of concerns. Certainly one of the major considerations will be cost. What impact will the cost of the screening process have on the net yield of the investment selected? Will it be so costly and time-consuming that it severely impacts the yield on the investments that ultimately comprise the results expected from the investment portfolio? Does the screening process require as an investment strategy an absolute adherence to the criteria? In order to increase the performance of the portfolio, is the investor willing to tolerate investments in companies that operate with less than 100 percent commitment to the social agenda?

A growing number of mutual fund companies are promoting social agenda funds. These range in size from the large multifund mutual fund families that offer one or a few socially responsible funds to the specialty firm whose fund promotes a specific social agenda. The individual investor can find track records and general fund objectives from a number of sources that are available in most brokerage offices or public libraries. Once a specific fund has been identified, the prospectus can be ordered, which will provide abundant detail regarding the fund's objectives, operating philosophy, historical track record, and individual investments. If these conform to the investor's stated social responsibility, an investment can be made.

If the socially responsible investor has a large portfolio, the services of a money manager may be in order. Finding a manager that operates or can create a portfolio that promotes the investor's social ideals may not be as easy a task as with mutual funds. The best source of information on this may be a charitable organization that promotes the same type of social agenda as the investor. Most likely, they have the organization's funds invested with a manager who does socially responsible screening. If not, they may know of managers who have approached them in this regard. Not all money managers, by any stretch of the imagination, offer these screening capabilities.

Once the correct manager is found, a portfolio can be structured for the investor favoring their particular social goals. A number of money managers offer some very effective screening processes. The costs associated with these extra endeavors are passed out to the investor, usually in the form of slightly increased management fees. On occasion, the money manager will structure a portfolio that allows for some deviation from a strict norm. This may be required in order to offer an investor a competitive market rate of return. This does not necessarily mean abandoning a socially responsible investing schematic, but rather slightly adapting to accomplish both a socially responsive goal and an investment result.

The third method of investing capital in socially responsible investments is for the investors to research and seek out the individual companies by themselves. This can be a time-consuming activity and one that does not guarantee that the companies selected will be as accurately researched as they would be by professionals. Personal satisfaction may be stronger with this methodology of investing, as the investments selected are more identified with the individual doing the picking and choosing. The rates of return, however, may suffer, as the pride of ownership may affect investment decisions.

Once socially conscious investors start to realize the impact that their current investable dollars can have upon the promotion of their own social agenda, the results can be significant. In coming to this realization, the individual social capitalist can become, from an investment standpoint, an activist. In so becoming, they learn that they do not have to wait until death to have their assets promote social good. It can occur while they are alive if they adopt this type of investment philosophy. This approach being adopted by even a small portion of the investing population can have a far-reaching impact.

SUMMARY

In a recent study, author and social philosopher Peter Drucker details what he terms "The age of social transformation."[2] He puts particular emphasis on the role that the nonprofit sector will have to assume as current and future social changes roll across our country. Their impact will be felt not only in social areas but in the political arena as well. As their responsibilities increase, so will their political import and impact. Would, for example, Americans continue to be as generous to charitable organizations if the income tax deductibility of charitable contributions were removed? What impact would a change in the tax-free status of organizations have on their ability to support their social activities? These and many other types of questions will arise as the financial resources at all levels of government are increasingly strained.

As government at all levels increasingly comes to grip with the constraints of current revenue-raising measures, as compared to the needs that require funding, the only logical place in which to resort is the nonprofit sector. As the remainder of this century winds downs and the next one commences, the needs of various communities and their constituencies will become more apparent as will the desire on the part of government officials to have the nonprofit organizations address these issues. In order to assure proper funding of these organizations, Congress must enhance the charitable giving sections of the tax code. Not only does that entail expansion of existing funding vehicles, it also entails the introduction of new tax-supported funding methods.

One of the other important areas that Drucker identifies is that of citizenship. The need to address feelings of alienation, of "not belonging," that has permeated many communities and age groups in our country. One enormously powerful force that can be created by the nonprofit sector is a reversal of this trend. By promoting volunteering on the part of many people, the nonprofit sector, will in turn, promote a new sense of citizenship. A new spirit will rekindle the American dream of neighbor helping neighbor and will begin to address the problems that today seem insurmountable but that if approached on an individual basis by concerned citizens are solvable.

As Ernest Becker so eloquently stated, "What man fears most is not so much extinction but, extinction with insignificance."[3] Those that adopt a social capital philosophy will not be insignificant.

NOTES

Chapter One

1. Robert H. Boemner, *American Philanthropy*, (Chicago: University of Chicago Press, 1960, 1988).
2. Robert H. Boemner, *American Philanthropy*.
3. Joseph Moeyman, "Freedom and Philanthropy," *Philanthropy Monthly*, October 1985, p. 35.
4. Trevor Smith, "An International Survey: Fiscal Treatment of Donors and Charities," *Philanthropy Monthly*, June 1986, pp. 24–25.
5. *The Chronicle of Philanthropy*, July 27, 1993, p. 34; *The Chronicle of Philanthropy*, February 9, 1993, p. 35.
6. *The Chronicle of Philanthropy*. May 1, 1994, p. 25.
7. Grant Williams, *The Chronicle of Philanthropy*. June 1,1993, p. 23.
8. Kristin A. Goss, *The Chronicle of Philanthropy*, February 9, 1993, p. 7; *Statistical Abstract of the United States*. 1992, U.S. Department of Commerce, Economics and Statistics Administration, Bureau of the Census.
9. 1992 Giving U.S.A., *1992 AATRC Trust for Philanthropy*.
10. Internal Revenue Code Sec. 644.
11. L. Brent Bozell III, *New York Post*, May 15, 1995, p. 19.

Chapter Two

1. IRC Sec. 170; IRC Sec. 642(c).
2. IRC Sec. 170(b)(1)(A); Reg. Sec. 1.170A-8(b).
3. IRC Sec. 170(b)(1)(A).
4. IRS Publication No.78 U.S. Government Printing Office, revised October 31 annually.
5. IRC Sec. 170(b)(1)(A).
6. IRC Sec. 170(b)(1)(C)(i); Reg. Sec. 1.170A-10(b)(1).
7. IRC Sec. 2055.
8. IRC Sec. 2522(a).
9. IRC Sec. 170(b)(1)(C)(i).

10. IRC Sec. 170(b)(1)(C)(i); Reg. Sec. 1.170A-8(d)(1).
11. IRC Sec. 170(b)(1)(C)(iii); Reg. Sec. 1.170A-8(d)(2).
12. IRC Sec. 170(b)(1)(C)(i); Reg. Sec. 1.170A-8(d)(1).
13. IRC Sec. 1011(b); Reg. Sec. 1.1011–2(a)(1).
14. Rev. Proc. 66–49, 1966–2 C.B. 1257; Rev. Proc. 79–24, 1979–1 C.B. 565.
15. IRC Sec. 170(e)(1)(B)(i).
16. Reg. Sec 1.170–13(c)(1)(i).
17. IRC Sec. 642(c)(5).
18. *Tax Economics of Charitable Giving*, Eleventh Edition, Arthur Andersen & Co., Chicago July, 1991.
19. IRC Sec. 1011(b) Reg. Sec. 1.1011–2(a)(1).
20. IRC Sec. 170(f)(2)(B).
21. IRC Secs. 170(f)(2)(B), 2055(e)(2)(B) & 2522(c)(2)(B).
22. IRC Sec. 673(a).
23. IRC Sec. 170(f)(3)(B)(i); Reg. Sec. 1.170A–7(b)(3).
24. Reg. Sec. 1.664–1(a)(1)(i).
25. IRC Sec. 664(d)(1).
26. IRC Sec. 644(d)(1)(A).
27. Rev. Rul. 77–374 1977–2C.B.329.
28. Reg. Sec. 20.2055–2(b).
29. IRC Sec. 664(d)(2).
30. IRC Sec. 664(d)(2)(A); Reg. Secs. 1.664–3(a)(1)(i)(a) & 1.664–3(a)(2)(i).
31. Reg. Secs. 1.664–3(a)(1)(i) & 1.664–3(a)(5)(ii).
32. IRC Sec. 664(d)(3)(A); Reg. Sec. 1.664–3(a)(1)(i)(b)(1).
33. IRC Sec. 664(d)(3)(B); Reg. Sec. 664(d)(3)(B); Reg Sec.1.664–3(a)(1)(i)(b)(2).

Chapter Four

1. IRC Sec. 644(d).
2. IRC Secs. 170(f)(2)(b), 2055(e)(2)(b), 2522(c)(2)(b), 642(c)(5).
3. Rev. Ruling 72–395 1972 c.b. 340.
4. Rev. Proc. 90–33 1990–25 i.r.b. 26.
5. IRC Sec. 170(b)(1)(a).

6. Cumulative list, organizations described in section 170 © of the Internal Revenue Code of 1986, IRS publication no. 78, U.S. Government Printing Office, Washington, D.C.,
   revised annually each October.
7. IRC Sec. 170(b)(1)(c)(iii); Reg. Sec. 1.170a-8(d)(2).
8. IRC Sec.. 1011(b); Reg. Sec. 1.1011–2(a)(1).
9. Reg. Secs. 1.1170a-1(c)(2); 25.2512–1; 20.2031–1(b); Rev. Rul. 68–69, 1968–1 c.b. 80.
10. Reg. Secs. 25.2512–2(b)(1); 20.2031–2(b)(1).
11. Reg. Secs. 20.2031–8(b)(1); 25.2512–6(b)(1).
12. Reg. Sec. 1.170a-13(c)(1)(i).
13. IRC Sec. 664(b).
14. IRC Sec. 170(e)(1); Reg. Sec. 1.170a-4(c)(1).
15. IRC Secs. 7520(a)(2); 7520(c)(3).
16. Actuarial values: alpha volume publication #1457;
    beta volume publication #1458; gamma volume publication #1459:
    U.S. Government Printing Office, Washington, D.C.
17. Rev. Rul. 60–370, 1960–2 c.b. 203.
18. IRC Sec. 2001(b)(1).
19. IRC Secs. 2523(a); 2056(a).
20. IRC Secs. 2505(a); 2010(a).
21. IRC Secs. 2523(i); 2056(d).
22. IRC Sec. 2523(b)(1).
23. IRC Secs. 2523(g)(1); 2056(b)(8)(a).
24. IRC Sec. 2503(b).
25. IRC Sec. 2513(a)(1).
26. IRC Sec. 2033 & 691(a); Reg. Sec. 20.2033–1 & 1.691(a)-2(a).
27. IRC Sec. 2056(b)(8)(a).

Chapter Five

1. IRC Sec. 2010.
2. IRC Sec. 2056(a).
3. *Estate of Power Crosley, Jr.* v. *Comm*, 47 JC 310(1966), Acq. 1967 CB2.
4. Reg. Sec. 1.664–1(a)(1)(i).
5. IRC Secs.509(a)(1), 509(a)(2), 509(a)(3) & 509(A)(4); Reg. Secs. 1.509(a)-1, (a)-2, (a)-3 and (a)-4.
6. IRC Sec. 2041(a).

Chapter Six

1. Elizabeth Greene, Stephen G. Greene, and Jennifer Moore, *The Chronicle of Philanthropy*, Nov. 16, 1993, "A Generation Prepares to Transfer Its Trillions," pp. 1,8,11,12.
2. IRC Secs. 301, 302, & 303.
3. IRC Sec. 1361.
4. IRC Sec. 4975(e)(7); ERISA Sec. 407(d)(6).
5. Reg. Sec. 1.61–9(c).
6. Robert B. Richardson TC Memo, 1984–595.
7. *Kinsey* v. *Comm*, 477 F.2d 1061(2d Cir. 1973); *Rushing* v. *Comm*, 441 F. 2d 593(5th Cir. 1971).
8. Reg. Sec. 1.664–1(a)(1)(i).
9. Rev. Rul. 67–137, 1967–1C.B.63.
10. Reg. Sec. 1.170A–13(c)(7)(ix).

Chapter Seven

1. Reg. Secs. 1.401(k)-(a)(4)(ii); 1.401(k)-(a)(4)(iii).
2. IRC Sec. 642(c)(5).
3. Reg. Sec. 1.664–3(a)(1)(i)(b)(2).
4. IRC Sec. 401(a)(9)(A); Reg. Secs.1.401(a)(9)–1, 1.401(a)(9)–1, B1 & B2.
5. IRS Notice 89–42, 1989–1 CB 683.
6. IRC Sec.3405(c)(1).
7. IRC Sec. 72(t).
8. IRC Sec. 3405(c).
9. TRA86 Sec. 1112(h)(3).
10. IRC Secs. 4980A(c)(1)(B) & 4980(d)(3).
11. IRC Secs. 4980A(c)(1)(B) & 4980A(d)(3).
12. TAMRA'88 Sec. 1011(A)(b)(13); TRA'86 Secs. 1122(h)(3), 1122(h)(5).
13. IRC Sec.401(a)(9); Reg. Sec. 1.401(a)(9)-1, B1.
14. IRC Sec.6018(a)(5); Reg. Sec. 54.4981 A-1T(c-7).
15. IRS Sec.402(e)(4).
16. Rev. Ruls. 60–31 1960–1 CB974; 69–474, 1969–2 CB105; 70–435, 1970–2CB100.
17. *Corporate Contributions 1990,* Anne Klepper New York: The Conference Board, 1992.

Chapter Eight

1. IRC Sec. 170(a)(3); Reg. Secs. 1.170-A-5(a)(1) & 1.664–3(d).
2. Private Letter Rulings 8042142, 7752099, 7809093 & 8037044.
3. Reg. Sec. 1.664–1(a)(3).
4. Rev. Rul. 77–73.
5. Reg. Sec. 1.1011–2(a)(3); Rev. Rul. 81–163.
6. IRC Secs. 170 (f)(3)(A), 2522(c)(2) & 2055(e)(2); Reg. Secs. 1.170A-7(a)(1), 25.2522(c)-3(c)(1)(i) & 20.2055–2(e)(1)(i).
7. IRC Secs. 170(f)(3)(B)(i), 2522(c)(2) & 2055(e)(2).
8. IRC Secs. 170(f)(3)(B)(i), 2522(c)(2) & 2055(e)(2).
9. IRC Secs. 170(f)(3)(B)(iii), 2522(c)(2) & 2055(e)(2).
10. Rev. Rul. 87–37, 1987–1 C.B. 295; Ltr. Rul. 8341009.
11. IRC Secs. 170(f)(2)(A), 2055(e)(2)(A) & 2522(c)(2)(A).
12. Reg. Sec. 1.170A-4(b)(3)(ii).
13. IRC Sec. 170(h)(1); Reg. Sec. 1.170A-14(a).
14. IRC Secs. 170(e)(1) & 1221.
15. IRC Sec. 170(a)(3); Reg. Secs. 1.170A-7(b)(1) & 1.170A-5(a)(2); James L. Winokur, 90 T. C. 733(1988), AcQ. 1989–1 C.B.1.
16. Rev. Rul. 73–610, 1973–2 C.B. 213.
17. Rev. Rul. 73–610, 1973–2 C.B. 213.
18. IRC Sec. 170(e)(1)(B)(i).
19. IRC Sec. 1361.
20. IRC Sec. 512(a)(2).
21. IRC Sec. 511(b).

Chapter Nine

1. Rev. Rul. 77–285, 1977–2 C.B. 213.
2. Rev. Rul. 77–285, 1977–2 C.B. 213; Ltr. Ruls. 7730015, 8839071 & 9048049.
3. IRC Sec. 664(d)(1)(A): Reg. Secs. 1.664–2(a)(1) &1.664–2(a)(2).
4. IRC Sec. 664(d)(2)(A); Reg. Secs. 1.664–3(a)(1)(i)(a) & 1.664–3(a)(2)(i).
5. Reg. Sec. 1.664–3(a)(1)(i)(b).
6. Reg. Sec. 1.664–3(a)(1)(i)(b)(2).
7. Reg. Sec. 1.664–3(a)(1)(i)(b).

8. Reg. Secs. 1.72–1(b) & 1.72–2(b).
9. IRC Sec. 72(u).
10. Ltr. Rul. 9009047.

Chapter Ten

1. *Eppa Hunton IV* v. *Comm.*, 1 TC 821(1943), *Ernst Behrend* v. *Comm.*, 23 BTA 1037(1931) Let. Ruls. 8708083 & 8304068.
2. IRC Sec. 170(E)(1)(A); Rev. Rul. 76–143, 1976–1 C.B.63.
3. Reg. Sec. 25.2512–6(a), Example 3.
4. Reg. Sec. 25.2512–6(a); Rev. Rul. 59–195, 1959–1 C.B.18.
5. Reg. Secs. 25.2512–6(a) & 20.2031–8(a)(2).
6. Let. Rul. 9147040.
7. Let. Rul. 7928014.
8. IRC Sec. 514(c)(1)(A).
9. Rev. Rul. 60–83, 1960–1 C.B. 157.
10. *Estate of Power Crosley, Jr.* v. *Comm.*, 47 TC 310(1966), Acq. 1967–2 C.B.2.
11. Rev. Rul. 64–328, 1964–2 C.B.11.
12. Ordinary life policy, issue age 45, Berkshire Life Insurance Co., Pittsfield Mass.
13. Ordinary life policy, issue age 45, Berkshire Life Insurance Co., Pittsfield, Mass.

Chapter Eleven

1. Rev. Rul. 77–385, 1977–2 C.B.331.
2. Reg. Sec. 1.664–3(a)(6)(iv).
3. Rev. Rul. 72–395, 1972–2 C.B.205; Ltr. Rul. 7929052.
4. Ltr. Rul. 7835037.
5. IRC Sec. 170(b)(1)(A).
6. Rev. Rul. 76–8, 1976–1 C.B.179.
7. Rev. Rul. 76–371, 1976–2 C. B.305.
8. Rev. Rul. 76–371, 1976–2 C.B. 305.
9. IRC Secs. 501(c)(3) & 509(a).
10. Rev. Proc. 82–39, supra note 3.
11. IRC Secs. 501(c)(3) & 509(a).

12. IRC Sec. 509(a).
13. IRC Secs. 170(c) & 509(a).
14. IRC Code Sec. 170(e)(5).
15. IRC Sec. 642(c)(5).
16. IRC Secs. 170(b)(1)(B) & 170(b)(1)(D)(i).
17. IRC Code Sec. 170(b)(1)(B).
18. IRC Code Sec. 170(b)(1)(D)(i).
19. IRC Code Secs. 4941(d)(1) & (2); Reg. Sec. 53.4941(d)-2.
20. IRC Code Sec. 4942; Reg. Sec. 53.4942(a)-1(a).
21. IRC Code Sec. 4945; Reg. Sec. 53.4945–1(a).
22. IRC Code Secs. 4941(d)(1) &(2); Reg. Sec. 53.4941(d)-2.
23. Jonathan J. Higuera, "Facing the Future," *Foundation News,* September–October 1992, pp. 27,28,29.
24. Jennifer Moore "An Increase in Gifts Pushes Assets of Community Foundations Up 11%," *The Chronicle of Philanthropy,* August 10, 1993, p. 8.
25. IRC Code Secs. 170(c)(2) & 170(b)(1)(A).

Chapter Twelve

1. Reg. Sec. 1.664–1(a)(1)(i).

Chapter Thirteen

1. Peter D. Kinder, Steven D. Lyndenberg, and Amy L. Domini, *Investing for Good: Making Money while Being Socially Responsible* (Cambridge, Mass: Harper Business, 1993).
2. Peter F. Drucker, "The Age of Social Transformation," *The Atlantic Monthly,* November 1994.
3. Ernest Becker, *Denial of Death* (New York: The Free Press, 1973).

Index